THE FORGIVE PROCESS

THE
FORGIVE
PROCESS

A LITTLE BOOK ON
Forgiving and Letting Go

LEE H. BAUCOM, PH.D.

NEW YORK

LONDON • NASHVILLE • MELBOURNE • VANCOUVER

THE FORGIVE PROCESS

Published in New York, New York, by Morgan James Publishing. Morgan James is a trademark of Morgan James, LLC. www.MorganJamesPublishing.com

The Morgan James Speakers Group can bring authors to your live event. For more information or to book an event visit The Morgan James Speakers Group at www.TheMorganJamesSpeakersGroup.com.

ISBN 9781683508977 paperback
ISBN 9781683508984 eBook
Library of Congress Control Number: 2017918800

Cover Design by:
Rachel Lopez
www.r2cdesign.com

Interior Design by:
Christopher Kirk
www.GFSstudio.com

In an effort to support local communities, raise awareness and funds, Morgan James Publishing donates a percentage of all book sales for the life of each book to Habitat for Humanity Peninsula and Greater Williamsburg.

Get involved today! Visit
www.MorganJamesBuilds.com

CONTENTS

Prologue
(A Parable)

When he was little, Billy was carefree. He was happy all the time and simply explored the world. It seemed boundless, and he felt boundless. Days started at first light and ended when it got dark. No worries. No struggles.

One day, Billy was playing with his best friend. They were having a carefree day, staring at the clouds passing overhead. As they were passing the time, Billy told his best friend a secret. It was not a huge secret. Just a little secret. One of those bonding moments between friends.

The next day, Billy was playing ball with all his friends. As it sometimes happens, an argument broke out about rules and who was right. Billy was winning the argument by popular decree. But the tide suddenly turned. Billy's opponent pointed at Billy and told everyone the secret Billy had entrusted to his friend. Everyone laughed. Except Billy.

Billy felt betrayed.

And Billy swore he would never let that happen again. Billy looked around and found a smooth stone. He wrote a note on it with the crayon in his pocket, "Never trust Tommy again." He slipped the smooth stone into his pocket, just to make sure he didn't forget.

Whenever Billy was tempted to tell Tommy another secret, he reached into his pocket and touched the rock. It reminded him of the dangers of telling secrets. Billy knew he was onto something — a system of protection, to make sure nothing hurt him.

A few days later, Billy's dad promised to throw a ball with him after work, just as he headed out the door. Unfortunately, things blew up at work and Dad got stuck. Billy was waiting on the front porch, watching for the car that was not appearing around the corner. "I guess it wasn't important to him," thought Billy. He picked up a rock beside him, found his crayon, and wrote, "Never count on what someone promises you." He stuck it in his pocket.

When his dad came home, Billy sat in his tree house and read comic books, and pretended he didn't hear his dad calling him.

Those rocks began to comfort Billy. When he walked, they jostled around in his pocket, reminding him that he had to be careful. Every now and then, he pulled them out and read the crayon writing, reminding himself that his "rules" kept him safe.

About a week later, Billy was playing in the field. Some other kids were rough-housing around. A sharp rock flew errantly, striking Billy on the elbow. It hurt. But there wasn't any real damage. The boys didn't even seem to notice.

Billy was hurt, but even more, he was angry that the boys didn't notice what they had done. He picked up the sharp rock, squeezed it hard, and said, "I won't forget you did that to me." Billy gripped it so hard that the edges dug into his hand. And several cuts on his hand bled just a bit.

This rock was harder to carry in his pocket. So Billy just carried it wrapped tightly in his hands, all the way home.

In his room, Billy grabbed a backpack and put the rock inside. He would keep it to remind himself of what those boys had done to him. Billy seemed to have missed the fact that those boys, after a while of tussling, gathered for a nice game of kickball. They went home, happy over a good day of play.

Billy took to carrying that backpack around with him, keeping his reminder rocks inside. The backpack was a bit cumbersome, but it seemed worth it to Billy, to remind him of his hurts. He reasoned that if he kept track of the events that hurt him, he could avoid them in the future.

So, it became a ritual for Billy. Whenever he felt hurt, he found a rock or stone, smooth or sharp, and made a note on it. Over time, the crayons faded a bit. It didn't matter, though. Billy would periodically take out each rock and remember what happened. Sometimes, it would be a little hard to remember the details, so he had to concentrate. But it was worth it to Billy. It was just the price of staying safe. That backpack was getting pretty heavy after a few years. But Bill kept at it. He kept the backpack with him, just in case he needed to refer to the stones.

One day, young Bill realized that he, too, made mistakes. He let others down. He let himself down. He wasn't doing all he felt he should be doing. Things he did; things he didn't do.

Bill started writing these things onto rocks, so he could remember to do it right the next time. He used a Sharpie for this project so the writing would be permanent. And the backpack became more than a bit cumbersome as Bill kept track of what he did wrong. So, he fashioned a sack to wear on his chest. Then, as he moved through his day, Bill could pull out a rock easily, and remember not to make that mistake again.

And as Bill grew older, he also wrote more details in his stone notes. That took bigger stones. But it was worth it, reasoned Bill, to keep track of the details. He didn't want to be hurt, and he didn't want to hurt others. It was, after all, an important thing. Who wants to hurt or be hurt? Not Bill.

It seemed that there was a never-ending number of things Bill would have to note. He would place a stone in his backpack and a stone in his chestpack, sometimes several per day.

Bill's back was achy every day. And to be honest, his shoulders were sagging under the weight of the rocks and stones. But Bill trudged on, reminding himself of the importance of his project. He believed that one day, he would no longer be hurt. And one day, he would no longer hurt another person.

Strangely, Bill never seemed to notice that the day that happened was never today. It was always "someday."

Then, one day, Bill couldn't move. It seemed that the last rock in the backpack and the last stone in the chestpack were just too much. Bill couldn't stand up and get off the bench. He had just stopped for a second, having just argued with someone. He was hurt, but he had also hurt the other person. A rock was added to each pack. And they were two rocks too many.

Bill tried to get up. But his legs would not budge the packs. Bill tried to get to the end of the bench, to gain a bit of momentum. But Bill could not get up. He was... stuck.

Fortunately, Bill was a smart guy. He knew he had to change something. So, he started looking for some rocks he could discard. He rummaged through his chestpack, thinking there had to be some rocks and stones he could throw away. But each time he looked at one, he said, "I can't let that one go. It is too important. I need to remember that." In the end, Bill left all the stones in his chestpack.

Bill then went through his backpack. One at a time, he pulled out a rock, remembered the incident, and felt a tremor of fear. He sure didn't want to forget THAT hurt, that moment. It would be bad to have that happen again. So each rock came out of his backpack but went right back in.

The sun was blazing that day, and Bill had no shade. He couldn't move, but he didn't want to leave his "treasures" there, either. So, Bill just sat.

As the day grew long, Bill decided he had to do something. He went through his bags again. But again, there was nothing he could leave out. Bill had built his life on those moments, using them to remind himself of who to avoid, what not to do, where not to go, and how not to act.

But mostly, Bill was working hard to not feel. To not feel the hurt from actions of others. To not feel the regret of hurting someone else. Bill had the best of intentions: don't hurt others and don't be hurt.

Bill was thoroughly stuck, unable to get off the bench. Unfortunately, that bench was far off the path, away from people.

Bill had no choice. He couldn't let go of his reminders. But he couldn't stay stuck forever. Bill was hot, tired, thirsty, alone. But mostly, he was exhausted. Carrying around those rocks and stones for years had worn Bill down.

At that moment, Bill thought back over his life. He thought of the times he had turned down offers to go to the movies, to go dancing, to go for walks, to go grab coffee. Those rocks were too heavy to take anywhere. So, he just avoided going anywhere they might get in the way.

He remembered friends telling him they couldn't hug him with those heavy, hard (and frankly, sharp) rocks on his chest and back. Of course, Bill didn't really believe them. He thought they just didn't like him. So, he would simply place another rock in his backpack.

Bill was alone.

Not just in that moment. But in life. He was stuck on the bench.

And he was stuck in life. If Bill could not let go, Bill would never be free. Bill needed to let go of the rocks in order to live.

INTRODUCTION

We all have "rocks" we have carried around, that weight us down and keep us stuck. We all have hurts we need release, to forgive. We all have caused hurts we need to release, to forgive ourselves.

Why does forgiving even matter? Some believe that revenge is best. That holding a grudge is protection. They believe forgiving is weak, misguided, forced, or even dangerous. As one person told me, "People just aren't built to forgive. I remember every hurt and slight. I refuse to let people take advantage of me." The result: she was stuck. Many others are stuck at that same point.

And other people are just not sure. Perhaps what happened just shouldn't be forgiven. Perhaps that person just does not deserve to be forgiven. There should be a penalty, they believe, to the actions that caused the hurt. Forgiving might be nice, but it might be a little too generous for the offender.

And many others would love to forgive; they just don't know how. They believe forgiving is a great concept — but it is only an abstract concept, perhaps even impossible to achieve. Just because you can't see a path, though, does not mean there isn't a path. You just need a light, and maybe a map, to see the path.

1

In my life as a coach and therapist, I realized very early on that we all need to forgive. We all need to have a way to release the hurts and slights. We all need to step away from the injuries that hold us back in life. For the most part, it is not a question of forgiving; the problem is a misunderstanding of forgiveness and the lack of a clear path.

In this short guide, I hope to help you fully understand forgiveness and to teach you the Forgive Process, so that you can find healing and release. More than that, I hope to show you how you can live more fully and be more engaged in life by forgiving.

Unreleased and unforgiven hurts hold us back and insulate us from fully living. Forgiveness frees us up and allows us to engage fully.

"Carl" came into my office with an open pronouncement: "I don't really believe in therapy, don't think you can help, and don't know why I am here." With that, he shook my hand and sat down.

"And yet," I noted the obvious, "here you are."

"Yep," Carl continued, "I am making everyone around me miserable. And to be honest, I am miserable, too."

I suggested that there might just be a part of Carl that believed therapy could be helpful; perhaps there was some small piece that saw potential and held hope. Grudgingly, Carl allowed that he had a bit of hope.

You may be a bit like Carl, wondering if something could help, if it is even possible to forgive. But to again note the obvious, here you are. There is a part of you that knows forgiving is the path forward, whether you trust it or not, whether you feel it or not, and whether you know how or not.

When "Sue" came into my office, she assured me that she had been hurt, but that as I would soon see, she should not be forgiving. She let me know that the hurts she suffered were so egregious that she should not forgive. In fact, she assured me, I would readily agree that she was doing well, given what had happened.

"And yet," I noted the obvious, "here you are. More than that, it would appear that the way you have been thinking and feeling is not helping."

"Well," Sue stated, "I am pretty miserable. I have a right to be. I just want to make sure there really is nothing I can do."

Like Sue, you may be convinced that the hurts done to you deserve no forgiveness; the people who hurt you should not be forgiven. And yet, there may be a part of you that is hoping to find a path to forgiving.

"Anne" found me during a break at a training session I was holding on the Forgive Process. I had seen that gait before, as she resolutely approached me, her stare boring down on me. She launched into her thoughts the moment she was in my conversational zone, "How DARE you! How DARE you tell me I should just forgive and move on. How DARE you tell me that I have to forgive. How DARE you tell me I have to let that person off the hook. Do you even KNOW what happened? You act like it doesn't matter what the person did, I still HAVE to forgive! Well, I won't!"

"Anne," I asked, "I'm wondering: we didn't hide the title of the session. You knew, coming in, that we were going to discuss the concept of forgiveness. And I am betting that you even knew, coming in, that I would actually be in favor of forgiving.

I would even bet, if you read the description of the training, that you knew I would give you a step-by-step process to work on forgiving. Is that fair?"

She sheepishly admitted that I was correct, that my assumptions were fair.

"And," I clarified, "At no point did I say you HAD to forgive, that you HAD to accept my assertions or follow my process." I paused.

Anne took a breath, relaxed a bit, and continued, "I just don't know if it is possible. I don't know if I want to or if I can."

"That is a different matter," I noted. I suggested to Anne that the process of forgiveness is quite simple. I also pointed out that as is true for many things, *simple* is far different than *easy*.

"But," I clarified, "there is no way for you to move through the Forgive Process if you do not believe that you would want to forgive. If you don't think forgiving would be helpful or healing, you won't go down the path."

She looked at me curiously. I told her that if I wanted her to travel across a desert, enduring the heat and dangers, I had better help her see a reason to cross the desert. I told her that my intention was first to explain why it would be useful to cross the desert — and what lay on the other side of the desert. I also told Anne that I intended to show her a map to get across the desert. I also promised to tell her how to cross the desert as safely as possible. But in the end, I assured Anne, she would have to choose whether to cross the desert or not.

Most people find themselves searching for help on how to forgive because they are pretty miserable. Perhaps they don't even know, like Carl, if the process could help at all. But, the pain of not forgiving is beginning to outweigh the pain of forgiving. The misery of not acting is outweighing the fears of acting.

Often, like Sue, people hold a secret belief that the hurt they have suffered is bad enough that they are either precluded from forgiving or that the other person doesn't deserve to be forgiven. They believe that the person should be held accountable, and our innocence is proof of this. Let me suggest that any belief that forgiving removes accountability is based on the wrong assumption. Any belief that not forgiving provides some sort of protection is also a wrong assumption.

There are few words so laden with assumptions (often false), beliefs, and emotions than "forgive." The word is weighted by cultural and religious beliefs. It is deeply tied into our hurts and pains. Many people tell me they know they "should" forgive, but don't feel like it is possible or fair.

The problem is in our assumptions and beliefs about the word. It is not the word, but our false beliefs about the word, that cause us problems.

WHAT IS FORGIVENESS?

What exactly is forgiveness? As you may have experienced, this is not so easily answered. Many words are simple to define; we all basically agree on the definitions. But *Forgive*, *Forgiveness*, and *Forgiving* are not such words. They hold emotional impact for us, and so we struggle with even defining them.

The Merriam-Webster dictionary makes it pretty clear, noting a few meanings: "to give up resentment of or claim to requital," "to grant relief from payment of," or "to cease to feel resentment against (an offender)." Pretty simple. You can forgive a debt or release a resentment for an offense.

And yet, we struggle with that. So, let's scratch a little deeper, perhaps into the origins of this word. The concept is quite old. "Forgive" derives from the Latin root of "perdonare." It passed through Germanic before coming into English. The Latin root, "perdonare," means "to forgive completely, without reservation." It is closely related to the word, "pardon." When someone is pardoned, they are released from the offense.

The Aramaic (and a closely related Hebrew) word "shbag," indicates forgiveness and means "to untie." Those older words give us some further guidance. We forgive completely so that we are untied from that event, injury, or insult.

The idea of forgiving is often caught up in "should's," though, which seems to trip people up. Likely, part of that is due to religious connections to the word. Many people experience religion as demanding that they *should* forgive, that there is a force behind it, a shaming in it. In other words, those religious structures leave people feeling that forgiveness is forced upon them — not as an opportunity, but as an obligation.

Perhaps some of our hang-ups are from childhood experiences where we felt forced to forgive. That would be the case for me. Well-meaning adults trying to teach us the idea of forgiveness might make it feel forced, perhaps not even experienced. Enforced forgiving rarely gets us very far.

My first memory of this is after yet another tussle with my brother. With only eighteen months between us, we could be the best of friends and the worst of enemies. My mother described us as rolling around like little bear cubs, sometimes playful and sometimes hurtful.

After one scrape-up, I remember my father's hands on each of our collars, standing us face-to-face. He first lectured us on family treating each other well. And then, he had each of us apologize to and forgive the other. I can tell you that I spoke the words, "I'm sorry," but no part of me felt it. I spoke the words, "I forgive you," but no part of me felt it. It was obligatory. I asked for forgiveness; I granted forgiveness. Per the requirements of the hand on my collar. Not as opportunity, but as obligation.

Many of us have similar events from childhood. We were forced to forgive, regardless of feeling.

"Alice" came to me in adulthood, still seething from childhood. She told me the story of an adult family friend who sexually assaulted her when she was twelve years old. She gathered all the courage she could muster and told her parents.

Her parents were supportive and wisely believed her as soon as she told them. Then her parents confronted the family friend. Alice was not present for this, so she stated she had no idea how that went. But Alice did remember the moment when her parents dragged Alice into the room with the offender. He looked at Alice, tried to give an excuse for his behavior, and managed an "I'm sorry." Alice stood staring at him, both seething in anger and terrified.

She said nothing.

Then her parents said, "Alice, he said he was sorry. You need to accept his apology and forgive him." Alice did not feel forgiving. She felt hurt and threatened.

She said nothing.

Her parents again pushed for Alice to forgive the offender. After an awkward and long conversation, Alice says she knew there was only one way to end the conversation. She looked at the man and said, "I forgive you." Alice remembers that at the same moment, her thought was, "I will NEVER forgive you."

Several decades later, Alice had kept that promise, and found herself still stuck in the pain of that event.

After sharing her story with me, she stared at me with raging intensity, "You can't tell me to forgive. I will not. I am still angry at him. I am angry at my parents. And if you tell me I have to forgive him, I will be angry with you."

"Alice," I started, "could I offer another thought?" She nodded. I continued, "I would never tell you that you *have* to forgive. But it occurs to me that every day, that man continues to rob your life and your relationships. That event continues to hurt you every day. You are still stuck there. Is that fair?"

Tearfully, Alice nodded in agreement.

"So," I added, "what if, instead of an obligation, you saw an opportunity? What if the option was to *choose* to forgive — when you are ready? It seems to me that you are here because you *don't* want to be captive to this. At some point, if that is correct, you have to find a way to put it — to put him — behind you. I would just suggest that choosing to forgive may be a significant part of that process."

Alice silently considered this. Then she told me, "I will not tell him I forgive him. I will not let him off the hook. I will not just let him think everything is all right."

"Fair," I responded, "you don't have to say anything to him. In fact, this isn't even about him."

Alice's softened gaze now looked confused.

Alice misunderstood forgiveness at its core. She believed that forgiving was for the other person. She thought it was a release for him. She missed an important point: It is not for the offender; it is for the offended.

Let me repeat that. You do not forgive *for* the person who hurt you. You forgive so that you are not held captive by the actions of another person. It does not free the other person. It frees you.

When my father had me by the collar, I had an opportunity to give up my anger toward my brother. It was not just to let him off the hook. It was an opportunity for me to get myself off the hook.

What keeps us from taking advantage of that opportunity? First, there are some myths of forgiveness that keep tripping us up.

MYTHS OF FORGIVING

It was the first night of a Forgive Process training class. We were gathered in a church room, whiteboard to my back. Sitting around the tables, people told me they came for various reasons. A few told me they didn't believe in forgiveness — but they would give me a chance to change their minds (always nice to start with a challenge).

Several others talked about their struggles with past events. Some dated back to childhood. Several were more recent, including marital betrayals. A few were horrific. One woman had a family member who had been murdered. Another was injured in an accident with a drunk driver.

After the introductions, I turned and wrote on the whiteboard, "What Are The 'Unforgiveables'?" I heard papers shuffle, but told them I wasn't quite ready to brainstorm yet. I just wanted to plant the seed.

Then, I went on to tell a story:

> "One day, you are hiking a trail in the mountains. You are lost in the beauty of the climb, amazed by the vistas that stretch out. You are minding your own business, just enjoying life. The trail is steep,

the mountain rising sharply to your side. The vista is off to your left, and your right side is close to the rocky mountainside. You hug the rocky area to stay on the narrow trail.

Somewhere above you, someone else is hiking. You can't even see them. But they dislodge a sharp rock. It careens down the side, bounces up, over, and down onto your shoulder. Lost in thought, you are jolted by the hit and pain from the cut inflicted. The rock lands at your feet.

After you rub your shoulder, wiping away the blood, you shift from pain to anger. You reach over and grab that stone. The sharp edges glisten a bit in the sun. You tighten your grip on the rock, raise it toward the upper trail, grip it tighter, and proclaim, 'I will not forget this. I will not let this go!' Holding tight, the edges of the rock cut into your hand. You continue your hike, committed to the climb. But, the joy is gone. Your shoulder is hurting. And now, your hand is also hurting. You now only have one hand to use in the climb.

Your climb is much longer, more difficult, far more painful, and robbed of any enjoyment.

Above you, the other climber continues the trek up and over the mountain, heading down the other side. Whether the climber knew of the rock, you can't be sure. Perhaps he kicked it over the edge. Perhaps he slipped and dislodged it. Perhaps he had picked it up to look at the glistening elements in the broken edges, then discarded it. And perhaps, he heard you below and decided to aim the rock toward the sound of you climbing.

In any account, he has continued his path over the top and has now begun the climb down the other side. He couldn't see what happened. He may even be unaware that the rock hit you (and even if he knew it, he doesn't know you have continued to grip the rock). He has gone on along his merry way.

You, on the other hand, fulfill your commitment to hold tight to the rock. By the time you finish your hike, your shoulder, while cut, is feeling better. Your hand, however, is throbbing, with cuts at multiple points along your palm. The muscles of your hand are cramped from the tight grip. You are in pain, possibly more from gripping that rock than from your shoulder."

I paused.

Then I added, "That is pretty much what happens when we refuse to forgive. The offense re-injures us, holds us back, and becomes another weight in life. Meanwhile, many times, the person you want to hold accountable is long gone, either unaware or uncaring of the damage done."

The room was quiet for a moment.

Then, one group member said, "So, what are you saying? We should just let the rock go? We get hit by the rock, and we don't do anything?"

"Ah," I replied, "that brings me to this question: What would you put in the 'unforgiveables' list of actions someone could do? These are the actions for which a person *should not* be forgiven."

The audience was rather creative and bold after a few minutes. Quickly, we had a list that included murder, rape, infidelity, harming a child, war crimes, and a myriad of other, rather horrible, actions.

As the offense list grew, I could feel the anger grow in the room. Interestingly, nothing had actually happened to the group — except that members were *thinking* about these horrible actions, and in some small way, feeling the need for justice.

Then I offered another thought: "What if forgiveness is for the offended, not the offender? What if the reason to forgive is so that you don't have to carry that hurt and injury with you indefinitely? What if forgiving had, primarily, nothing to do with the offender?"

Myth #1: Forgiveness is for the Offender

This, I believe, is the first major block to people forgiving. They think that they *should* forgive, perhaps because it would help the offender somehow. They make forgiving about the offender.

Forgiving is for the offended. Not the offender. It may or may not change the relationship between the offender and the offended. But primarily, it frees the offended from the offense, the hurt, and the pain from the event. It also can free the offended from the offender.

To be clear, it is possible that forgiving frees someone up to re-establish a broken relationship. But it doesn't have to. It always frees up the forgiver to live more fully. The future of the relationship is a separate decision.

When "Mark" and "Jane" visited my office, the hurt from Jane was palpable, although it took on the appearance of venomous anger. Mark hugged his end of the couch while Jane spoke to me, while glaring at him.

Jane told me that after 18 years of marriage, she had discovered a three-year affair that only ended because Mark had been caught. That was six months ago, and nothing had shifted during that time. There was zero communication during the day, both hard at work in their careers. Their two children were busy in high school, with both Mark and Jane doing what they could to make sure the bases were covered in the family.

When Mark hit the door, it was usually after Jane was home. The verbal barbs started when he came in, sarcasm and accusations flying, kids present or not. Mark's phone was confiscated and searched at the door. His social media accounts were checked later that evening. Not surprisingly, nothing was found on either, given the expected scrutiny.

You might be wondering why they were in my office.

As it turns out, Mark finally one day said, "I can't keep doing this. I am sorry for what I did. I apologized. I have tried to make things better. But you clearly hate me and are constantly mean to me. I don't want to live in fear of coming home. I'm moving out."

Jane, not skipping a beat, said, "You stole three years from me. I've only had six months. Of course you are leaving. You've been gone for years."

With all the calm he could muster, Mark said, "I love you. I screwed up. I am a bad person. I get that. I would love for us to work this out. Clearly, you don't. That is why I am leaving."

At that moment, something strange was happening in their relationship. Mark was the one who broke the boundaries of his marriage. But Jane had since stepped in to continue the destruction of the relationship.

Jane stopped and asked, "Could we talk to someone?" Mark agreed. Thus, they were in my office.

There was one major problem in our sessions: the anger from Jane was endless. Let me point out that anger is a secondary emotion to hurt. Anger is what we often express when we are feeling hurt. But the anger can often do a very good job of hiding the hurt.

And Jane was not very interested in letting the anger go. When I approached the hurt in a conversation, Jane would get tearful and then lash out again, reigniting the anger. Sometimes, anger is easier to feel than the hurt beneath it.

After a few rather ineffective sessions, I asked Jane if she would return alone. Jane turned her icy glare to me. "So," she hissed, "Mark is the one who screws around, and you want to make this my fault?"

"Nope," I responded. "Mark messed up. And Mark seems to be repentant about that. Jane, I am not asking you to come here to blame you, but for the possibility of making progress…

if we can move past the hurt and anger. At this point, you are holding the hurt and anger. Not Mark."

She exclaimed, "I have to 'get over this' so *we* can get over this?"

"Not entirely incorrect," I said. Jane wasn't sure whether to respond in anger or confusion. I continued, "Jane, before you could possibly make a decision about your marriage, you have to make a decision about forgiveness. You have to decide whether you can even begin to forgive. Then — and only then — can you make a decision about the marriage. I don't know. You may decide *not* to forgive. That is your choice. I just don't see a way to move forward until that is decided."

Jane and I worked together for several sessions. During that time, Jane began to see how holding onto Mark's infidelity was costing her. She thought she was holding Mark accountable, making him pay the price. While that was not entirely untrue, the real hostage was Jane. Every day, she spent hours re-living the painful moments of discovery. She poured over the evidence she had. She rethought all the details she had pried from Mark. Jane's entire day was lost in an affair that had long ended.

When Mark was coming in the door, Jane was caught in an emotional state from a day of *remembered trauma*. The trauma was in the past, but it was yanked into the present on a daily basis. When Mark arrived home, Jane was loaded with emotions — mainly hurt and anger — and it gushed out onto Mark.

I knew that as long as Jane stoked that fire of hurt, anger, and resentment, she would continue to torch their relationship, along with Mark and herself.

In our first session, just the two of us, Jane asked, "So, you want me to just let this go? Let him off the hook? You think Mark deserves for me to forgive him?"

"Jane," I asserted, "this is where you have it twisted. I do hope to see you forgive Mark. And it is possible that the two of you will heal your relationship. But that is the wrong direction. This is for you. Forgiveness allows you to move forward in your life, no longer held hostage by someone else's actions and choices. You forgive so that you can move forward. It is for you — not Mark."

But Jane struggled back. "You think I must forgive Mark, right?"

"Nope."

"So you think it is okay for me to not forgive him, then, right?"

"Nope."

Jane was quiet. Then she admitted, "I have been thinking that I am required to forgive him, that it is my responsibility. My faith talks about this every week."

I wanted to make sure Jane got this one: "Jane, I am not sure what your faith tells you each week. I just know that forgiving allows **you** to move forward. Forgiving is for **your** benefit. It might help the relationship. It might help the offender, in this case, your husband. But primarily, it starts the healing process for you."

Over the next few weeks, Jane and I began working through the Forgive Process.

Myth #2: Forgiving Lets the Offender Off the Hook

Closely related to the belief that forgiving is for the offender is the belief that it removes responsibility.

"Jack" spent his childhood at the mercy of an angry step-father who abused both Jack and Jack's mother. Jack's biological father left the family when Jack was a toddler. When Jack started school, his mother started a new relationship. At first, "Ralph" seemed great. He played ball with Jack, took the family to the movies, and seemed to make Jack's mother happy.

That lasted just a few months. A couple of beers in the evening began to expand to a six-pack. Within six months of Ralph moving in, nightly television had the added spectacle of Ralph mixing drinks on the coffee table. A few drinks in and Ralph was happy to tell Jack what a pain he was, that he always needed something else, that he was just taking Ralph's money. Soon, Ralph made it clear that Jack and his mother were just out to take advantage of Ralph.

Soon after that, Ralph was grabbing Jack to make his point. Then, Ralph began to smack and hit Jack to punctuate his point. At school, Jack tried to hide the bruises. Having seen his mother lonely and sad before Ralph, Jack tried hard not to offend Ralph. He feared his anger, but he also feared Ralph leaving.

Between them, Jack and his mom did all they could to stay away from the house on weekends. And they tried not to upset Ralph during the week. Neither strategy worked well.

When Jack was 17, Ralph grabbed Jack's mother and threatened her. All of Jack's anger from over a decade of abuse poured out. He took Ralph to the ground and made it clear that there was never to be a hand placed on his mother, ever again.

Ralph moved out the next day but caused legal upheaval for years after. In fact, Ralph committed himself to breaking Jack's mother, emotionally and financially. Ralph stayed out of reach. Jack seethed with anger for years.

When Jack came to see me, he was bitter and angry. Jack was struggling with his career and had begun to numb his frustrations with alcohol. After a bar fight over nothing, Jack realized his anger was misguided. Worse yet, he was becoming Ralph. So he sought help.

"Jack," I started, after hearing his story, "it might be time to forgive."

That was like pouring gas on the fire. Jack erupted, "I will NEVER forgive that man! He robbed me of my childhood. He left my mother miserable. And you want me to just let him off the hook?"

"Nope."

"But, you said I needed to forgive him," Ralph tried to clarify.

"Yep." I continued, "Jack, forgiving him doesn't let him off the hook. In fact, you might forgive him and let him know, but you might just forgive him. On your own."

Jack quietly responded after a thoughtful pause, "I'm listening."

I told Jack about Pope John Paul II's assassination attempt. Mehmet Ali Ağca shot the Pope four times as the Pope entered St. Peter's Square. It almost ended the Pope's life. After he had recovered, Pope John Paul went to visit Ağca in his prison cell, to forgive him.

Jack quickly jumped in, "So, he let him off the hook?"

"No, Jack," I answered, "he did visit to let him know he was forgiven. But he also left Ağca in his jail cell to face the consequences of his behavior." I continued, "Jack, you don't even need to visit Ralph. Forgiving him does not let him off the hook; it releases you from the hook."

Over the next few months, Jack and I worked through the Forgive Process.

Myth #3: You Have to Forgive and Forget

This myth tends to roll off people's tongues. "Just forgive and forget." I have heard many people say it, and I was also convinced they never considered how that might happen.

If an event is traumatic, it is unlikely to be forgotten. To take it a step further, if you forget something, it probably was slight enough that you didn't need to work on forgiving. Forgiving is what you do when you are caught by the actions of another person and find yourself anchored to that event. (There is another layer of forgiving, "Everyday Forgiveness," that we will discuss later.)

We struggle to forgive the big things, the events and actions you are unlikely to forget.

Interestingly, I rarely hear the offended person speaking the words, "forgive and forget." Often, it is either the offender or some related person wishing the situation would simply evaporate. To "forget" means to somehow arrive at a space where the event never happened, at least in your mind.

"Sherry" came to visit me shortly after the holidays. Her older brother had constantly tormented Sherry as a child. He called her names, belittled her, and often physically threatened or mistreated her. Sherry still had several scars from being shoved down. But most of the wounds were emotional and largely invisible.

When Sherry left for college, she cut off most ties with her brother but did maintain a connection with her parents. Only at holidays did the siblings' paths cross.

This particular holiday season, Sherry and her family gathered with her brother and his family at their parents' home. While Norman Rockwell may have been able to capture a great portrait of the family, just below the surface was a decades-old conflict simmering.

At one point during dinner, Sherry's brother told a story about a childhood incident, but when it got to the point that he shoved Sherry off of a retaining wall, leading to a broken ankle, he chalked it up to an uncoordinated sister who stumbled.

Sherry erupted. She stood up, pointed her finger at her brother, and told him he had stolen her childhood. She continued, voice filled with fury, that she spent every waking day in fear of him, feeling bad about herself, and wanting to run away. Sherry's parents tried to intervene. But Sherry was ready for that, too. She turned on them and questioned, through tears, why they never protected her, why they always sided with the brother, and why they always wanted a family get-together.

The table was silent. Then her brother started, "I — I — it wasn't like that! I didn't hurt you. It was you. When I did do something, you started it...."

Sherry screamed, "Stop it! You are a liar. You always have been. You always wanted it to be my fault. But it just wasn't. You were a bully, and you still are!"

At that point, Sherry's mother tried to calm the situation, saying "Sherry, that was years ago. It is over and done. You need to forgive and forget."

Sherry was silent. That night, Sherry and her husband packed up with their kids and returned home. But Sherry felt all the childhood wounds reopened.

Which is why she came to see me.

Sherry was feeling a bit confused. Could her mother be right?

But she was also angry. Why should her brother be freed from his actions? How could Sherry forget?

After telling me the story, I said, "Sherry, your mother is half right." She glared at me. I was teetering on becoming the enemy.

"Sherry," I continued, "it is clear how deep the hurt is and how strongly it is gripping you. I think you do need to forgive so that you are free from that hurt and pain. But forgetting — that seems pretty impossible."

"Well," Sherry assured me, "if I can't forget it, I probably can't forgive it."

I sat with her through several moments of silence. Then, she looked up at me and asked, "Right?"

"No. I don't think so."

Sherry's mother had repeated that phrase so many times that Sherry thought maybe she was right, and that was why there would be no forgiveness. "So, if I can't forget it, how can I forgive it?"

I suggested, "What if you thought about it differently? Not like you pretend the events happened differently than they did, but the circumstances might have a different understanding. Perhaps you could think about your brother differently."

"No!" asserted Sherry. "I refuse to downplay what he did."

"Sherry," I assured her, "this is not about downplaying. That would be more in the realm of pretending or forgetting. But what if, at the end of forgiving, you have a slightly different view of him? Right now, he is pure evil in your mind. There might just be something else there. Someone else there."

Forgiving is not about forgetting. But it is often about remembering (and understanding) things differently, seeing the actors and events from a different perspective. And often, forgiving leads to empathy and acceptance. That can change the viewpoint (note that I said "can," not "will").

To summarize, forgiving is not FOR the other person. It does not let that person off the hook. And you are not required to somehow forget what happened. Forgiving, however, is FOR you, the forgiver. It allows you to get off of the painful hook. It allows you to redefine who YOU are, and it may just redefine the events — not forgetting them but understanding them from a different perspective.

All of that might sound like a good idea. So why is it we struggle so much with forgiving?

WHY WE STRUGGLE WITH FORGIVING

I was in the middle of a conference on forgiving when a hand shot up. Somewhere between accusatory and curious, the participant asked, "If forgiveness is so good for you, then why is it so hard? Why don't we just forgive?"

"Great question," I responded, "because it would seem that if it were good for us, we would jump right in, right? Except that doesn't seem to be the case in many areas of life. We know we should exercise on a regular basis, but the vast majority of people don't. We know we should eat healthy foods and avoid unhealthy foods. Except most people don't. We know we should get a good night's sleep. Except most people don't. In other words, just because it is good for us doesn't mean we automatically do it."

I went on to explain that there are a couple of reasons why we don't forgive quickly or easily. And if you want to move to forgiveness, it is often good to understand what is behind the resistance. It is also good to notice when you do it easily. We often fail to notice that.

For example, let's say that a close friend is clearly in a bad mood, focused on some crisis in their own life. On that day, in a conversation, you share something. Your friend's response is reactive, harsh, and hurtful. It stings.

At that moment, you walk away angry and hurt (reminder: anger is a secondary emotion to hurt). You stew on it for a bit. Then, in a moment of clarity, you remember your friend's crisis. You remember your friend was already in a bad mood. Your perspective changes. You realize that your friend's response had far less to do with you and far more to do with your friend. So, you forgive; you release the hurt fairly quickly, maybe even with a bit more empathy for your friend.

My guess is that you have done this countless times in your life. And it will happen countless times in the future. Living with people means that there are frictions that happen, points where you rub each other a little raw.

In fact, I consider this to be "Everyday Forgiveness" — when we forgive people for those small slights and hurts which proximity causes. You may quickly forgive a spouse who says something thoughtlessly, especially after a bad day. Or you might forgive a friend who forgets an event, given a busy or hectic life. You just let it go, partly because you understand "these things happen," or because you know about that person's life circumstances.

Remember, there are already times when you readily forgive because you naturally make a shift, you see things — the other person, the events and circumstances, and perhaps yourself — differently.

The crux of the question is *why* we don't forgive *when* we don't forgive, since those are the times that stick with us and hold us captive.

There are three central reasons that we struggle to forgive. These reasons are important to identify and understand, so they don't hold you back in your process. Forgiving is so important that you need to understand what holds you back. One reason we fail to forgive is easy to see, so let's start there.

Reason #1: Our Survival Brain Holds Onto "Threats"

Your brain has a primary function: survival. Before anything else — before you build relationships, do great things, and change the world — you have to survive.

Your brain is a survival machine. At least one part of your brain is built specifically for that. It is both the most primitive part of your brain and the quickest to respond.

That was great in a time when mortal danger awaited our ancestors behind every tree, rock, and hill. In order to survive, our ancestor's brain needed to be on high alert, ready for defensive or evasive action just to avoid being something's dinner or someone's captive.

While there are far fewer such threats (notice that I didn't say there were no threats), your primitive brain still has the survival imprint from millennia ago. And it hijacks the rest of you every day.

Bosses, coworkers, friends, spouses, and family members are unlikely to pose a mortal threat (and if they do, you need to take a very serious look at your world and change it). Yet, our brains go on defensive, protective, survival mode with little provocation.

This threat assessment is not a logical or sensible assessment. It is often automatic and instinctual. And while it would be useful if your survival brain would do some post-threat assessment ("Was that tone of voice, facial expression, or body language a threat? Nope. So I won't react that way next time"), the brain launches into threat-mode the very next time.

Every slight risk of threat puts this part of your brain on alert. And this primitive part of your brain then puts the rest of you on alert. You might get used to it, but you still react. A boss's upset yelling? Your body gets a hit of adrenaline. A spouse's cross words? Your body goes into threat mode.

In terms of survival, it is far better if our brain *over*-responds than if it under-responds. Survival requires being "on guard," getting out of the way, and remembering the trigger for being "on guard" and getting out of the way. In other words, it is about holding on to the memories of times you feel threatened.

What works for survival, though, can keep you from thriving. Unchecked, that survival brain sees threats everywhere and remembers past threats every time.

I say "unchecked," because once you know what that part of your brain is doing, you can opt to not be constantly "on guard." If you know the reason behind why you struggle to forgive, you can accept the protective nature without allowing it to rule.

Just by wiring, this part of the brain remembers and catalogs the threats (and the people your brain views as a threat), automatically reminding the rest of your brain and body when those memories are stirred. When on automatic, it seems safer to not release those memories. This makes us feel like we should not forgive — it just seems to be a threat to survival.

But, it isn't.

Oh, and just because you choose to forgive does not mean you won't be aware of the threat. That part of your brain just can't be shut down. But, it also doesn't need all that space in your mind. Threats and forgiveness operate on different planes.

Reason #2: We Believe Life Should Be Fair

Our five-year-old mind still lurks in our head and believes life should be fair. Think back, if you have kids, to their childhood. If you don't have children, think back in your own life. Remember those episodes of that child stomping a foot and yelling, "This isn't fair!"

It is a normal developmental stage to believe in fairness. That little belief system lives on in us, even with evidence to the contrary, that life *should* be fair. So when life doesn't feel fair, we can have a strong emotional response. We stomp our feet, declare "Life isn't fair," and demand fairness.

(Notice that the whole fairness thing for that child is tied to "fair to ME," and not so much about extending fairness to others. That belief survives into adulthood for many people.)

But life isn't fair, is it? Some people suffer for little reason, and others profit for little reason. Some struggle with health issues in spite of their efforts, while others are healthy in spite of their poor choices. Some people are born into affluence and privilege, while others are born into poverty and powerlessness. Through no fault or choice of their own. Just the role of the genetic dice.

And beneath this "Life Should Be Fair" belief is a hope that "There Should Always Be Justice" — which is usually based in justice from the point of view of the person holding it. In other words, fairness is also about wanting justice — even if it is a "justice" that matches a personal definition of that word. But justice isn't always a part of life. Just like life isn't fair, there are many times when there is no justice — at least from an individual's perspective.

Sometimes, people refuse to forgive because they are waiting for a return to fairness. They are waiting for the scales to be re-weighted, for things to even out. Then, they could forgive. Which is great, if life were fair, if there were always justice.

Life isn't fair. And forgiveness does not always include compensation for the hurt. When people wait for *fairness* or *justice*, they often end up waiting in misery. Caught in a false belief that serves only to keep you stuck.

Or you can give it up and move forward.

Reason #3: People Don't Have A Process

The other day, I was at a conference. At lunchtime, we headed off to eat, and I sat down with a couple of other guys in attendance. As we ordered, one of my colleagues mentioned he was intentionally trying to eat better. Our meal the night before was a bit, well, rich — especially the very decadent chocolate cake at the end. My colleague said he was trying to get back on-track.

Since I try to be intentional about eating healthily, I asked if he was following a particular plan, or if he was just trying to make better choices. He noted a particular popular diet. This led to a discussion about the differences between our food choices (really, not much).

We both ordered the same lunch, both staying true to our eating style. So he chose the lunch because he had a plan, a format. It was fairly easy to look through the menu and eliminate all the things that fell outside the parameters (most things) and choose from the remaining (a few things). Easy. Because he had a template, a plan.

But then we talked exercise. My friend admitted that he was not doing well with that one. He said he would go into his community's recreation room and was overwhelmed with the equipment. He just did the treadmill for a bit and left. "I wish I knew more," he told me, "but it just seems too complicated."

I responded, "I bet I can simplify it in about five minutes. Mind if I try?" He was open to that. So, I gave him a few parameters I used, including using resistance training (weights), not so that he would be in any bodybuilding contests, but so that he would stop any natural muscle loss that happens from the aging process.

Within about ten minutes (it took me longer than I predicted) of conversation, he had an exercise plan that was pretty simple. This new plan, though, allowed him to work his entire body with just a few exercises that hit the major muscle groups. He realized that he could shorten his treadmill time by a few minutes and then hit another piece of equipment, do a few resistance exercises, and have a full workout.

The difference between his eating choices and his exercise habits was less about motivation and more about understanding. He had a plan for one, but was overwhelmed with the other. Given some familial health issues, he was motivated — he just didn't have the information he needed to have a process.

If you are reading this book, you likely have the motivation. You are unlikely to be reading this book for fun or curiosity. You are likely here because you know you need to forgive (you are motivated) but you don't know how (you lack a process). In the following chapters, we will solve the issue of process.

Let's delve into the process. It is not complicated. There are only six steps in the Forgive Process. Some may be a bit of a challenge. But the challenge will be more about mindset than action. And if you find that some steps meld into each other, that's fine. Remember, this is a process, with less distinction between steps than what I note as I explain the process.

It is kind of like doing two exercises with the same weights in your hand. The weights didn't change. Only the direction of the resistance and the muscles used.

If you find yourself stuck on one step, go to the next one. With the exception of the first step (you DO need to get through the first step), the other steps will build on each other. Try to follow a linear path. But if one has you stuck, sneak a peek at the next step. Then, return to where you were stuck and see if it has loosened a bit.

Ready?

Let's get started.

STEP 1:
DECIDE TO FORGIVE

It all starts here. It's the simplest step. But that doesn't make it easy.

Sometimes, people buy a book for a little entertainment. Sometimes, people buy a book for a little knowledge or understanding. My guess is you bought this book because something has you stuck. Or to put it more clearly, you are stuck.

Unless it was just a curiosity read, you are here because something happened and you are trying to get beyond it. There is someone and/or something that you need to forgive. And you want some guidance on how to do it.

But just because you think (or even know) you need to forgive, that does not mean you have decided to do it. Right now, you may be on the fence, unsure if you can or will forgive. Or you may have committed to the *need* to forgive. But that is still different than *deciding* to forgive.

Or maybe you are already past this hurdle. You may have already made the decision to forgive. If so, this step is covered. Still, let's be sure.

The first step is simply a decision to forgive. Not just a decision to act okay, not just a decision that you need to forgive. It is a decision *to* forgive.

"Debbie" came to see me after attending a workshop I taught at her church on forgiveness. Over the course of several weeks in the workshop, she shot questions at me, throwing them at me over a fairly skeptical gaze. She seemed engaged and interested, but unconvinced.

After a couple of weeks of stewing on the training, Debbie made an appointment. When she sat down, she hugged her coat up against herself, clearly holding a barrier between us. It was also clear that the skepticism was still between us. And yet, she was in my office, sitting on the edge of the couch. Something was going on.

"Debbie," I invited, "I appreciated your questions during the training. It was clear you were processing things and working on your own thoughts. I was glad when you called to schedule. I'm guessing something is going on with you. Where can we start?"

With a slight pause, Debbie started, "I truly do want to let this go and move on. But you can't think I will just let him off the hook! It isn't fair for him to do what he has done, then walk away. It is pretty unfair that I have to forgive when he was the bad guy."

During that session, Debbie shared her broken heart. She married, right out of college, to the only boy she ever dated, from high school through college. They were "that couple," according to Debbie; the couple everyone thought was perfect. And it seemed that way to Debbie, too.

They married, he started his career, and they started a family. Three children in, Debbie thought everything was okay. They both had their interests and friends, they traveled, and they chased their children through busy schedules. "Oh, sure," Debbie told me, "the connection wasn't great." But she just thought they were on "pause" (not knowing there is no such thing in a relationship).

Debbie discovered the affair when she received an "accidental" email. Her husband confessed, said he was not in love anymore, and wanted a divorce — all within an hour of a tearful and angry discussion. The next day, he packed up and moved out.

Over the course of the next few months, Debbie tried desperately to convince her husband to return. Most attempts started in expressing hurt and ended in angry accusations. And each time, her husband exclaimed that "This is why I can't stay in the marriage."

Over the next couple of years, they divorced, went to court repeatedly for custody and monetary issues, and continued to deteriorate. While originally repentant, Debbie's husband turned to attack. He hid assets, manipulated friends and family, and worked to isolate Debbie. On several occasions, Debbie ended up hospitalized, convinced that she was really as bad as her husband made her feel. She was broken.

"So now, after all that, you think I should just forgive him. You think I should just let him off the hook," Debbie concluded.

Anger and hurt are powerful cement for events. They lock them into our psyche and soul, keeping the pain pumping long after the events have unfolded.

I suggested, "Debbie, your ex is long gone. He doesn't communicate with you. He has let himself off the hook. Your anger and hurt do nothing to him. But they certainly do damage to you. I am not suggesting you should forgive him, as much as I am inviting you to consider forgiving him — for you."

Debbie, hands covering her face, sobbed. Her shoulders heaved up and down with the tears.

After a long time, Debbie told me she knew I was right, but she didn't know how to do it.

"Knowledge is the easy part," I told her, "the struggle is in doing it. But the start is very simple. The hard part is behind you when you know you need to do it, when you acknowledge it is time. The simple next step is to decide to forgive."

"That's it?" Debbie accused. "That's what you want me to do? Just *decide* to forgive?"

"Debbie, that is a big step. It is not a 'just.' Think about that word, 'decide.' It means, literally, 'to kill away the other options.' When you fully decide, there is no other option left. You commit to stepping forward. You commit to that action. And it is not a small action. For you, this has been over a decade of hurt and anger. You have been captive to the story and to the thoughts about what happened. When you decide to forgive, you will see that you are letting go of those thoughts that have defined you. It isn't about forgetting them. But you must release them so that you aren't captive to them."

We sat silently as Debbie processed this.

Over the years, I have come to see that this first step seems simple to many people, leading them to gloss over it. Later, as they move forward, they realize they had not committed fully to forgiving. In order to really move forward, you must truly and fully commit to forgiving, even without knowing the next steps.

When Debbie had processed my words, she looked up at me, her face more resolute and firm, her eyes clear and bright. "I am ready. I've been waiting all these years for something from him. An apology. Remorse. Something. Anything. What I have been doing is not working. You are right. He is gone. He isn't feeling any of the pain I feel. He isn't suffering. I am ready. I decide to forgive him. I do."

What about you? Are you ready to take that step? You may not quite be ready to decide. This isn't a step I take lightly. While it may seem elementary, it requires commitment, resoluteness.

When my son turned eighteen, he and I went skydiving. We drove out to the middle of nowhere, got some small amount of instruction, and hopped on a plane for a tandem jump with an instructor. Already, I had made some choices: I agreed to skydive. I was going to go to the skydiving location, listen to the instructions, suit up, and climb into that plane.

But to be honest, none of those decisions were difficult. They had no consequences. I could always change my mind. I could always back out.

The plane taxied through the field, and we were airborne. As we climbed into the sky, I knew I could still say no. We could still turn around.

My instructor strapped me in. Still, I could say no.

We opened the door. I looked down at the tiny farmhouses below. I could still say no.

At that moment, I was aware that I had not fully decided. I could still say no.

The instructor yelled the same instructions in my ear, one more time. Still, I could say no, I could back out.

Then he asked, "Are you ready?"

Decision time. There was no going back. We leap or we don't. My choice. Until we actually let go. Now was the decision. I took a deep breath, turned, and said, "Yep." We shoved ourselves out of the plane.

I had decided.

Up until now, you may have been on the fence. You probably know you need to forgive. Otherwise, you wouldn't be here. You may be ready to let go and move forward. You may want to feel better.

Are you ready to forgive? Decision time.

The first step is "simply" to decide to forgive. Simple choice, simple decision, simple action. That doesn't mean it's easy. Simple is not the same as easy.

Sometimes, we start to define ourselves by those painful moments of the past. For some, the person or the event may have even become our identity. We do that sometimes. We suffer a painful event(s) and absorb that as who we are.

"Had a bad childhood."

"Suffered a horrific crime."

"Married to an abuser or cheater."

"(Your choice of identity)"

Oh, the list could go on and on. But, I want to make this clear: deciding to forgive does not mean something didn't happen to you. It simply means you are ready to move on from it, no longer defined by the event.

When an event defines us, we stop choosing our own definition of ourselves. We chain ourselves to events and people, to hurt and pain, and we become anchored, trapped by the events or people.

Yes, that event, person, or moment may have defined you. I would simply ask whether that definition expands you or diminishes you. Life seeks expansion. When you aren't expanding into life, you are trapped in pain, uncomfortable but unsure how to move forward.

If you find yourself not quite ready to decide, that is fine. You are not being forced into forgiving. At some point, when you are ready, you will want to drop the chains and move forward. The Forgive Process will wait for you.

But if you are done with the hurt, tired of being stuck, the first step is realizing that those chains holding you are held by you. Decide to release them.

Or perhaps, back to my skydiving, trust the parachute and shove yourself out the door.

Decide and jump.

And then, it is time for the next step in the Process. You are about to put on your reporter's hat. Ready?

STEP 2:
ENEMY TO EMPATHY—SEE THE PERSON AS HUMAN

"That monster stole my childhood!" Anne stormed.

I agreed. "Anne" lived through an abusive and frightening childhood. Her father was violent, angry, vengeful, and controlling. The mood in the house completely turned at 4:30 p.m. every day. That last hour before her father came home would be the last peaceful moment until he left the next morning.

Anne's father hit the door angry and was looking for a target. Anne's mother, in an attempt to calm him, met him at the door with a beer. Proving not to be a good drunk every night, Anne's father became sloppy angry after several beers. He broke furniture on a regular basis, slapped Anne's mother, shook Anne, and threatened everyone.

Every morning, Anne was happy to escape to school. She was a straight A student, reveling in the calm and support of her teachers. It was the only place where Anne felt loved. At home, everyone was focused on surviving and avoiding injury. At school, Anne sought approval through her work and attitude.

Later, Anne's efforts were aimed at getting out of her home and into college. In spite of her father's assertions that Anne would amount to nothing, "like her mother," Anne saw her chance. She graduated at the top of her high school class and received a full scholarship. From there, Anne made sure she rarely had to go home.

In fact, for the most part, Anne never looked back. She would call her mother and beg her to leave her father. But she pretty much avoided home as much as possible. When her mother's pleas and guilting lured Anne back home, mostly on holidays, Anne's father quickly reminded her of why she stayed away.

Anne finished college at the top of her class and followed up with law school. Then, right out of law school, she became a public prosecutor and specialized in domestic violence.

For the most part, Anne felt she had escaped her childhood. Until Anne's mother called her late one night to let her know her father had suffered a massive heart attack, was in the ICU, and would probably not survive. Anne left immediately to support her mother but had no intention of seeing her father.

After lots of begging, Anne's mother convinced Anne to go to her father's bedside. Anne told me that throughout her childhood, her father looked like a tightly wound spring, ready to pop at any point. Even drunk, he always seemed on the verge of flying out of his chair, propelled by anger, toward anyone in the room.

With wires and tubes connected to him, he looked more like a deflated balloon, more sunken into the bed than having any clear shape. And he looked terrified.

No matter, thought Anne, he deserved this. She secretly wished for years that he would die, leaving Anne and the family in peace. But now, she was faced with that reality, and Anne found the smallest bit of conflict within herself. Anne's father dominated so much of her thoughts — not in loving ways.

Barely audible, Anne's father looked up and said, "I'm sorry." Anne knew what she heard, but refused to accept the words. "NO!" she exclaimed. She fled the room, nearly tripping over a nurse coming into the room. She didn't stop until she was at the elevator. Even as she stood there, Anne heard the "stat" call to his room. Anne stood in the hall for a few minutes, summoning several elevators, only to let them close without her.

Anne knew. Her father died less than half an hour after whispering those words.

"He was a monster. I never had a pleasant moment with him. He was never kind, never affectionate, and never supportive. So what am I supposed to do? Just forget all that and forgive him?"

"Anne," I started, "you can't just forget. That isn't possible. You don't need to, though. In fact, what I am about to ask of you is far beyond that. It is to consider something else." I paused.

"I don't like the sound of this," Anne guardedly told me.

My request of Anne was simple. I asked her to do some background research. "Play the part of a reporter, trying to gather information on a subject. What was his background? Who was he and what made him?"

Anne and I discussed this for a few moments before Anne admitted this was part of her legal training. When she took classes in defending a client, the first thing she learned was to get behind the action and to the person — to learn about the person. The hope was to "humanize" the defendant to the jury.

My own background training is in Systems Theory, especially as applied to family systems. In culture, we often like to look at a single person, in micro-focus. That is the approach of individual therapy models. It is what we learn in Psychology 101.

In Family Therapy 101, we discover that all of us live in a web of relationships that form us. Our early relationships shape us and direct our actions. And many of our actions come in reaction to others in that web — at least until we become aware of this and decide to not let that web pull us around.

I remember sitting in a room, hearing the lecture, and realizing the implications. "Fault" became a little less sure. Multi-generational impacts became much more clear. While some might point to their parents for some issue or hurt, the parents had parents. And those parents had parents. And those parents had parents. And... well, you get the idea.

Another point became very clear in my studies: hurtful people have been hurt. Hurtful actions come out of hurt.

> CLARITY POINT: This process is NOT about excusing the person from their actions. It is about understanding the actions in context. It turns out that "mean" people have a history of how they got there. This is not so much about the actions as the actor. There can still be consequences. But there can also be understanding of context.

Several weeks passed before I heard from Anne. In fact, I had begun to wonder if I had chased her off. Perhaps she was not ready for the process. Maybe she was too rooted in her hurt to take it on right now.

Then the phone rang, and Anne rescheduled.

The Anne that came into my office for that second visit was far different than the one who first visited. Her presence was lighter, more relaxed, and far less angry. Her brow was not quite so etched.

Anne sat quietly for a few minutes. Then she began to tell me about her research. Anne spent that month calling friends and family. She pieced together the story of her father. She looked up at me and said, "By the time he was my father, he was broken. I had no idea."

As Anne dug in, she discovered her grandfather had been a heavy drinker and was very abusive. Several times, he broke ribs and arms of his children, including Anne's father. According to family members, Anne's grandfather died still spitting venom. And it appeared that Anne's father caught more of the abuse than others. He repeatedly stood up to his father and paid for it. Until he was drafted and sent to Vietnam.

While in Vietnam, Anne's father fought in some of the worst battles. Anne discovered that her father watched several friends die right beside him in a horrible fire fight. According to those around him, Anne's father never spoke about what happened. They only knew through others. As it turned out, Anne's father bravely fought to save and protect his platoon.

There were many other episodes of hurt and pain. And Anne gathered each as a puzzle piece into her father and who he was. She finished the biography and looked up at me.

"I get it. I understand his anger and hurt," Anne said. "But I don't see how that excuses what he did to me. I just understand he was hurting — and I guess it came out in anger."

"Anne," I told her, "this was not about excusing your father. It was about understanding your father. We tend to turn those who hurt us into a caricature that rarely truly represents them as a full human being. It reduces them to their worst moments. It ignores the moments that made them, formed them, into that person. That was all I wanted for you. To see him a bit more fully, with a little more reality and a bit more understanding."

Anne sat quietly.

"I'm wondering," I continued, "you seem a bit more relaxed, a bit less angry. Is that accurate?" Anne nodded. I offered, "I think that in the process of learning about your father, you discovered he was actually human. What he did to you was horrible. Why he acted so angrily is tragic. People are often more complicated than we want them to be when we see only their bad moments."

Interestingly, we all want to be seen for the "why's" and not the "what's." We want to be understood for why we do what we do, over what we did. Which is why people, in the midst of justifying an action, don't speak to the action but the circumstances around the action.

Many times, I watch a couple do this dance: "I can't believe what you did!" "Well, I did that because _____." "You are going to blame me for that? I did that because you _____." And on and on. If fact, left to their own devices, I am pretty sure they would track the conflict back to the moment when they met!

Each is pointing to the actions of the other, but justifying their own actions. That's what we do. We humanize ourselves and dehumanize others.

Social scientists have a term for this: Attribution Error. The Attribution Error basically says that if I do something wrong, I see it as a mistake. If you do the same thing wrong, I see it as a character flaw. I let myself off the same hook I sink into you.

We all have a story, and we all do hurtful things. Step two is about context; not about the hurtful actions, but about the context of the hurtful person. Empathy is an awareness of the context of the other person.

Does this mean that you need to put on your "reporter's hat" and dig into the story of that person? Do you need to discover the context of the person who hurt you?

Maybe.

But not necessarily. In the abstract, we all know what I just said. We just tend to carve out an exception for the person who hurts us. You can likely acknowledge that something is going on inside that person. However, you might stop short of empathy. But what if you extend empathy to that person? Even in the abstract. Even without knowing exactly why, but just because you know people have a story of their own.

I have a core belief that people do the best they can, *given where they are*. That belief includes you and me. It also includes people who hurt you.

So let me clarify this belief. It is not that I believe people are always operating at their optimal level. I don't believe that we are always at our best. But I do believe, given what is going on in life at a particular moment, we do the best we can.

Never, not once, have I had someone tell me, "I am just not doing what I can; I'm not trying to do well." Okay, admittedly, sometimes people are overly harsh on themselves and will say the words. But even that comes from a struggle to do better. As they process it, they discover they are doing the best they can — and wanting to do better.

Let me state the belief again: ***People do the best they can, given where they are.*** Right now. And at prior times. It might be better later, but right now, it is the best they can do.

When I look back on events (from a different perspective), it is often clear I could have done better. I could have acted, reacted, or responded differently. Why didn't I? Because I was doing the best I could, from where I was then. That doesn't mean I just shrug it off, excuse myself, and move on. I often see places where I need to be accountable for my actions, where I need to apologize and accept responsibility.

We live in a blame culture. Someone has to be blamed. And generally, we don't want to be the ones blamed. That makes it easy to want to pin it on someone else and let them be solely to blame. This isn't about blame, but understanding. It is an understanding that people simply do the best they can, given where they are. In an hour, a day, a week, a month, a year, they may be at a different place and will act differently.

The sticking point for this belief is that we often want others to act better than they can, at any particular time. We want people to be at a better place than they are. We expect them to be different. The struggle is to accept they are really doing the best they can, where they are.

> *CLARITY POINT: This belief that people do they best they can does not negate consequences for behavior. Actions do have consequences, both in terms of natural laws and the legal system. They also have relational consequences. The belief that people do the best they can, where they are, is shared not to excuse the behavior, but to realize they are/were acting due to their own circumstances. I am not excusing behavior as much as building a path to forgiving the person for those behaviors.*

ACTION STEP: Seek to see the person as human. See the actions as coming from their own struggles. Remember that hurting comes from hurt. You don't have to research the person's biography (although you can) in order to build empathy. You simply need to make sure you see that person as a human, struggling through life, as we all do. It is the risk of acknowledging we all can be hurtful, and we all are doing the best we can, given where we are. Even the person you are forgiving.

Building empathy and understanding may create some shifts within you. And you may resist, feeling that you are just letting them off the hook, giving them a free pass, or even excusing their behavior. You are not. I am not suggesting this as a step to necessarily re-establish a relationship. At this point, we are loosening the chains of hurt, so that you can forgive and release.

You may find that thoughts and memories pop up, gripping you tight. You may even notice thoughts you have not had in a long time, memories you had not remembered for a long time.

The next step is how you deal with those thoughts and memories, so they don't continue to bounce around within you, keeping you both stuck and in pain.

STEP 3:
Breathe and Release—
Let The Memories Pass

Momentum is a powerful force. Once something is moving in a direction, it tends to gain more and more momentum. It is like a stone dislodged that starts rolling down a hill, faster and faster. And like a snowball rolling, it grows larger as it moves.

When something happens, that event passes. But we often add momentum with other thoughts. Those thoughts add more energy. Someone does something to you. You begin to think about it and begin to add attributions to that other person. You start to remember other events through the lens of your hurt. You see other slights and injustices. You begin to see that person as more and more hurtful. You see the events as more and more unfair. Momentum grows; as it builds, the object is harder and harder to stop.

When I was in college, for a short time I drove an old car with a manual transmission. One day, that old battery was dead, and I was stranded. Since I had push-started cars before (high school friends with old cars found themselves stuck sometimes), I knew I could get it going. It wasn't a big car, so I reasoned I could get it rolling, jump in, pop the clutch, and be off.

On a slight decline, I started pushing. At first, it was pretty tough to get the car rolling, so I shoved from a deeper crouch. I lost my footing just as the car started rolling. It left me behind, rolling faster and faster. I got back to my feet and ran after it, first pulling at the door to slow it down. What was hard to get rolling was now impossible to stop simply by grabbing it. The car had momentum. I let go of the door, ran harder, and jumped into the front seat. At that point, I was no longer trying to control the car from the outside; I was at the controls again. Almost out of room, I managed to pop the clutch, start the engine, and hit the brakes. I was at the bottom of the empty parking lot, almost into the road. Momentum had taken over.

The same thing happens when something painful occurs. The event gains a bit of momentum. Our thoughts about it, fueling our emotions, add energy and momentum. It starts rolling faster and faster. At that point, we have a hard time stopping. It just has too much momentum—at least, until we decide to get out of the way.

In retrospect, I have come to realize that the car was far less valuable than my life. I was fortunate not to have caused an accident. I was foolish to pursue the car, to try to stop it. The car and I turned out just fine, but many times, momentum ends badly.

When you are struggling with a painful event — something that is holding you back — forgiving is deciding to let it keep on rolling. The difficulty is in the decision to quit chasing, to quit trying to change the events.

The ancient Greeks believed in the Fates, three sisters who determined what happened to people — when they were born, how long they lived, and when they died. They called the shots, regardless of human action. We use the word "fatalism" to describe having no choice in what happens. When someone is "fatalistic," they believe they have little volition in choosing the outcome. Events, as interpreted by such people, are unavoidable and unalterable.

I don't believe in fatalism. I do believe we have a role in determining what happens, given the events we can't control. Yes, we are all headed for the same "fate." We will all die. But how we make choices during events in life does determine our path through life. We get to make choices and direct our lives, within the constraints of external events.

Interestingly, though, our culture struggles with letting loose of what has already happened. We want to change the past. While I don't believe in fatalism, I am a fan of "reverse fatalism." In other words, we accept that what has happened has happened. Events in our past are in the past. They cannot be changed or altered.

Often, people struggle with trying to "redo" that past, to think through it long enough and hard enough to find a reality where the events didn't happen. In fact, this is one thing that keeps us trapped and struggling to forgive.

Debbie kept going over it in her mind, thinking of how her marriage could have been different: "If only I had been more loving." "If that other woman had not come into his office." "If he had not left the marriage." "If I had not argued and fought with him." And on and on. The re-working of the past, struggling to redo it, is part of what kept the wound so fresh for Debbie.

Part of the process of Debbie deciding to forgive was to decide that what happened was in the past, done and over. There was no redo. It was a matter of moving forward and accepting what is.

Sometimes, it is a struggle to accept what is. And one reason is because of one word, one simple question: "Why?" It calls for an answer — even when there often is no answer. At least, there is not one that satisfies or quiets the question.

Early in my career, I was a hospital chaplain. Most days were spent between the world of elation when surgeries were successful, outcomes were positive, and babies were born healthy, and the world of despair when diagnoses were bad, surgeries failed, and accidents happened. Being the chaplain, I was often handed the theological question of "Why?"

Along the way, I realized that while some people asked "Why?" as a theological question, there was another layer to the question. "Why?" was also a question of "How could this *not* have happened?" It was a struggle with What Is. It was an attempt to rewrite what happened.

Partly, this was just a desire to wake up from a bad dream and discover a world where there had been no accident or illness. And partly, it was the very human desire to problem-solve the situation out of existence. Patients and family members desperately tried to find a way around the tragedy, to find a way to redo things.

(Interestingly, people rarely asked "Why?" when things turned out for the better. The question only emerged in the face of tragedy.)

This also comes out in "if only's." These thoughts focus on trying to find an alternative way for things to have gone, "if only" something had been different. Unfortunately, things weren't different, and circumstances were exactly as they were. And they have already happened.

"If only the driver had stopped," they would say, "If only I had not smoked," "If only the doctor had been better," "If only I hadn't ignored that symptom," "If only...." This is the struggle with What Is. It becomes a struggle to find a different *Is*. It is an attempt to find a way to redo things that have already happened.

Notice how often we return to the "why's" and "if only's" of those past events. It isn't only immediately after the event. It continues well into the future, repeatedly.

Thoughts and memories have a way of recirculating. It is what our mind does. It creates thoughts, mulls over things, tries to problem-solve — which is great if it is a problem that can be solved.

But that same process can trip you up and hold you down if those thoughts are really trying to undo what can't be undone, redo what can't be redone. That was the nature of my chaplain discussions. People were caught up in trying to redo the done. They were trying to find a way to take control of the uncontrollable.

Do you do that? Do you find yourself revisiting a past event, trying to figure out how to make it happen differently, or even keep it from happening at all? Maybe you don't think you do, until you consider that question of "Why?" If you find yourself caught on "Why did this happen?" I would challenge you to consider the *possibility* you are really trying to find a "redo."

Let's return to that subject of thoughts. I have discussed this in my two earlier books, *Thrive Principles* and *The Immutable Laws Of Living*. We humans are blessed and cursed with a thinking mind capable of language. As I sit and write this in the early morning hours, I am actively thinking, using language to try to communicate an idea.

As I tell stories, I am re-living those stories through my memories. Those memories are thoughts I have recalled (and as I noted earlier, not with precise accuracy). I recalled them because I had a language context, a reference point. I could think, "remember Debbie," "remember Alice," "remember that car." And in an instant, I can pull those memories into my awareness.

This is a pretty amazing trick if you are reminiscing. But it has a pretty painful capacity when the memories are about past hurts. That recall system is partly to help keep us safe by remembering dangerous situations from the past.

I'm just guessing here, but I doubt a wildebeest walks up to a watering hole thinking, "Boy, I'd better be careful here. Just the other day, Hank was getting a drink, and a lion jumped him." Sure, he is wary at the watering hole because that threat portion of the brain is aware the area is dangerous. But let me take it one step further. I am betting that wildebeest, when away from that watering hole, has little capacity of even recalling what happened there. In other words, I don't think it can *choose* to ponder that moment at the watering hole. It might flash across in images. But not by conscious recall.

Which is different for you and me. If I were to ask you to recall the last time someone really hurt your feelings, you would likely recall it fairly quickly. You could probably start telling me about it, even as the memory of it started flowing. Soon, your body would be responding as if it had just happened. You might get tearful, maybe a little angry. You might even tell me about that great comeback line you thought of — after it was over.

Language has that capacity. It is a gift and a curse. We get to remember the highlights and low points, and the moments in between, just by recalling them.

And sometimes, we don't even choose to recall. Something triggers the memory. A word, sound, taste, smell, feel — something triggers our senses, and our mind instantly recalls that moment, that memory. This is still part of that threat detection system. Many times, the threat is long gone and not an issue, but once the thought is recalled, we often tend to stick with it for a bit, returning to our language capacity to keep it alive in our mind.

Which leads us back to this challenge of forgiving. And it happens in two ways.

First, people often keep replaying those moments of hurt, trying to find a redo. It is an attempt to make the bad stuff not happen. So, you might recall those moments that keep you stuck as a way to find an alternate ending. To find another way where you weren't hurt, where it didn't happen, where the offender didn't offend.

Second, people often have triggers that recall those memories, almost without volition. You see something, hear something, smell something, even taste or feel something, and the memory floods back. Our senses have the capacity of tying us to those memories.

But what happens next, in both cases, is interesting: we "process" it. We turn that memory over and over, examining it from angle after angle, re-living it more and more. The more we examine it, the more vivid it becomes. The more vivid it becomes, the more central it feels. And it begins to drag us down.

Surfers know that one of the dangers of the bigger waves is being pinned to the bottom. You can be riding a wave one moment, then in the next moment, wipe out and find yourself rolling on the ocean floor, pinned by crashing wave after crashing wave of a "set." Usually, you are out of breath from surfing, making this a pretty dangerous scenario.

Memories of hurtful events can do that to us. One moment, we are riding the waves of life. The next moment, a memory catches us by surprise, and we find ourselves pinned down by memory after memory rolling over us, holding us under.

While the feelings can be similar, there is a difference. Waves of water are heavy; waves of thought are weightless, except for the weight we give them.

Thoughts are thoughts. They are created, and they dissipate. I often have an idea hit me while I am in the shower. Not a convenient place to think about something useful. My wife is fairly used to seeing me tear through the room with a towel, trailing water as I get to my smartphone or some paper to write the thought down.

Why am I in such a hurry to record that thought? Because I know it won't stay long. Thoughts come and go. (And I am pretty sure the thoughts I fail to write down were probably my best thoughts ever. At least that's what I tell myself.)

Thoughts will stay around for a while when we give them energy and attention. That term, "entertaining a thought," is so telling. The thought is getting my energy. I am building it, growing it, making it stronger and stronger. The more energy I give, the more energy the thought gains. It sucks up energy, quickly becoming a "thought storm."

Oh, and memories? They are thoughts about and from the perceived past, dragged into the present. Let's just group memories and thoughts into the same category: thoughts.

Then we can divide those thoughts into "useful" and "not useful." Not "right" and "wrong." Rather, it's just a question of whether a thought serves me or harms me.

Some people struggle with this, but those memories we hold so tight, as a way of "keeping safe" — they aren't exact. They are imperfect recordings of those events. And they are contaminated by the continued thinking about the events.

A few years back, my family was gathered around a Thanksgiving meal, telling stories. My brother and I were talking about the exact same event. But from each of our retellings, there is no way you would know it was the same event. We remembered very different details and a very different chain of events. And yet, we both were there. We both experienced it. Our memories simply didn't match with each other. And my guess is that neither of our memories matched what actually happened.

CLARITY POINT: This is not to say that what happened to you is "all in your head." It is to clarify that the memories you have of what happened are not entirely accurate. They are not perfectly recorded and recalled.

And, more importantly, even if they were 100% accurate, they are memories.

Which are thoughts.

And thoughts do not have to hold us captive. Thoughts have the power we give them. I know it doesn't feel that way when they are gripping you. But just think of all the thoughts and memories that have passed and been lost.

Memories and thoughts can (and do) pass. Unless we dig into them.

Which brings us to this action step: Breathe and Release. Let the memories pass.

There are actually a couple of steps to this. The first is a simple step — again, this should not be confused with "easy." This step is simply to accept that what happened *has* happened. This is about *accepting What Is*. No need to try to redo or undo. Accept that whatever happened did, indeed, happen. (Which is still different than assuming your memories of what happened are 100% accurate.)

The second step is to stop wrestling with the memories. You might wrestle with memories, hoping to get rid of them (but you're really only giving them energy and strength). Or you might wrestle with memories in an attempt to find a better outcome (see above to accept What Is). Or you may wrestle with the memories as a way of reminding yourself of what happened, who you are, and who that other person is. In that process, you are choosing to define yourself by that moment. When anyone does this, they become the result of that event, losing the broader context of life.

> *COACHING POINT: If you find yourself uncomfortable or even angry with what I just said, notice this. It is incredibly important. That anger is telling you a piece of identity has been tied to the event. At this point, some people are quick to tell me I am asking them to pretend that something didn't happen. They often think I am trying to "erase" the event, or even reduce the tragedy of what happened.*
>
> *This is not at all the case. In fact, I am very much in favor of recognizing What Is, not trying to redo or undo. But I am also in favor of not being stuck, not being trapped by what happened. It's like anchoring your boat, then pretending to try and sail away. You may look like you are moving, but the anchor line keeps you right there.*
>
> *Forgiving is not about pretending it didn't happen. It is simply choosing to no longer be tethered to an offense or offender. It is choosing to move forward into a bigger life.*

Likewise, I am not a fan of being defined by any one event in your life. We are all bigger than a single event (even a big one). We have way more to offer to the world. And our identity is so much broader and deeper than any one event or era in our lives.

Which brings us back to this process of breathing and releasing. Notice what happens when a memory hits you. Sometimes, it catches hold, reverberating around within. It might start as just a triggered memory. But it can quickly take over your senses, causing you to vividly recall the sights, sounds, and sensations. That is why those memories can have such a hold on us. They can seem to be happening again at the moment you recall them.

You can't stop the trigger, the starting point of the remembering. But what happens next, you do have some options — at least once you start practicing. Generally, we add energy to those painful memories, searching for more details, more sensations. This isn't because you want to re-live it, but because the memories have hijacked your brain.

I don't believe we are designed to do this with memories. I think this ancient remnant of protection is misused by humans. This is a design feature that reminds you of potential danger.

The design flaw is us holding onto that same memory (that thought). Once you are alert to potential danger, the next step would be to let it wash over and out. To let the memory release.

This is different than what we do: stoke the memory. From an ember to a flame, and often to an inferno.

The linchpin between stoking and releasing a memory? Your breath. Well, your breathing. Your breathing is either a *fear-accelerant* or a *fear-suppressor*.

Remember our discussion about that fear center in your brain? It is so ancient that it does not understand words. It is a pre-verbal part of your brain. Yes, you can activate it by thinking back, "Remember that time _____ happened, that was really scary?" The words of recall are not what trigger the fear response. It is the memories experienced. Which is why that experience tends to build.

If I think back to a time when I was attacked on the street, just the recalling of that event does not start my fear response. It is when I recall the images, which then starts a process of recalling the sounds, the feelings of that evening, and the injuries inflicted. I can make those images vivid. And as I do, my body begins to go "on alert," as if the threat is here, now. My adrenaline builds; my body gets prepared to fight. Not because of my thinking, "remember that attack," but because of the memories I recall and re-live.

One very important thing happens when anyone starts thinking about traumatic, painful, or hurtful events: our breathing changes. Even as I sit here typing, only barely recalling that event, I can feel my stomach has tightened. My abdominal muscles tightened up to protect my vital organs — from a remembered incident, not one happening now.

Remember, the fear part of your brain cannot tell the difference between a real event and an imagined event. It experiences both as happening now. We go into "fight/flight" response — ready to either fight or get away from something

— even if you are like me, sitting alone (well, with a dog sleeping by my chair) in a kitchen, very safe. (This is why many people enjoy scary movies or action movies. Our brain reacts as if it is happening, causing a response in our body. It is also why some people find those same movies a bit too stimulating.)

Once your body is on alert, your breathing automatically shifts to your chest. But your deepest breaths come from your diaphragm. It doesn't have a bunch of bones (your ribs) keeping it from expanding. But it also doesn't have a protective cage (your ribs) to protect the organs. So, the abdominal muscles tighten, constrict, and protect.

At that point, when you go on alert for any reason, your breathing comes from the top of the chest. This happens automatically. And as long as you keep up that breathing pattern, your fear brain thinks it is unsafe. So, it keeps your body on alert. This causes a feedback loop: chest breathing leads to fight/flight, which leads to chest breathing, which leads to — well, you get the point.

Time to make a conscious choice and short-circuit this. Don't underestimate the power of shifting your breathing. I have used it with patients in the hospital to manage pain and end anxiety attacks; I have used it in therapy sessions to help people shift away from fearful, anxious moments, and as a way to shift out of traumatic memories. The process taps into the body's natural systems of returning to calm.

If you have tried yoga, taken singing lessons, or sat in meditation, you may have already learned the technique (it's then just a matter of applying it). I call it "belly breathing." It is simply diaphragmatic breathing — shifting your breaths to where they belong, in your diaphragm, your belly.

The nice thing is how easy this skill is to learn. The tough thing is practicing it. Your breathing, with just a little anxiety, shifts to your chest. And most of us have been taught to stand up straight and hold in our stomach — in other words, restrict the diaphragm.

Breathing is an interesting thing. You do it automatically, without giving it a thought. But you can also choose to take over control. Much of the day, you are unaware it is going on. It just happens (good thing). You don't spend your time telling yourself to "breathe in, breathe out, breathe in, breathe out." But you could. In fact, now that you are reading this, you are probably quite aware of your breathing.

The reason this is important is because you can then choose your breathing pattern if you need to change it. While I wouldn't suggest it, breathing rapidly through your chest is likely to raise your anxiety level. Instead, I would recommend breathing deeply through your belly, which lowers your anxiety level.

If you are not familiar with belly breathing, let's take a moment to get the hang of it. You are far better equipped to practice and learn it now than when you need it later.

The easiest way to learn (or relearn) this breathing method is to do it lying down on a bed, the floor, or a couch. It just needs to be somewhere you can be flat on your back.

Okay, the next step is nearly as difficult: Place a hand over your belly button and the other hand on your breast bone, right in the middle of your chest. Easy, right?

Now, take a breath in, focusing the breath so that only the hand on your belly button rises and falls. You draw the breath in with your diaphragm (a muscle at the top of your stomach, which draws downward). The hand on your chest should remain still, as should your shoulders. Be sure to consciously relax your abdominals when you do this. Otherwise, you are forcing air in where it does not want to expand. It only works with relaxed belly muscles.

Practice it until you feel the difference and aren't struggling to keep your chest hand still.

Then, practice it standing up.

Then, practice it sitting down.

You can belly breathe when you are in the car, at work, eating meals, walking (even running, with some practice), and when you are trying to fall asleep in bed. Once you have it down, you don't need to have your hands on your chest and belly. But there are times when I am really struggling with that fight/flight response that I still place my hand on my belly, just to remind myself to breathe there.

If you want a perfect model of this, watch a little baby sleeping on its back. Watch the baby's belly go up and down. The baby has it mastered because that is how we naturally breathe. If you forgot how, it's just a matter of remembering and rediscovering. Your lungs will thank you. Think of the process as rhythmic: slow breath in, slight hold, slow breath out, slight hold, repeat.

You may be wondering why breathing matters to forgiving. Remember those memories? They fuel your difficulties with moving forward. When a hurtful, painful memory arises, that deep fear brain believes it is happening, and your body reacts as if it is happening. Your breathing probably constricts to your chest, driving the fear and anxiety. Which reminds you of how dangerous and threatening the memory seems. And it reminds you to **not** forgive, to **not** release.

Even if you have chosen to forgive and release.

Unless you make a conscious shift.

The choice to forgive has been made. The desire to release is there. So, you make a conscious shift to belly breathing when the memories pop up (and they will). That gives the body a chance to discover something crucial: the memories are not a threat. They may be memories of threats, but they no longer threaten you. Memories lose their power when we take back the power. The fuel for hurtful, painful memories is anxiety.

The anxiety allows the brain to continue keeping us on alert, thus "demonstrating" the importance of the memory. But once the anxiety is disconnected from the memory, the body calms, and the brain follows.

COACHING POINT: If you are like most people, you want this to happen instantaneously. It would be nice if you learned to belly breathe, applied it the next time a memory hit, and the memory shifts.

And that might happen.

But if you are like most people, you have created a "thought habit" around that memory. It is likely that when a hurtful memory hits you, you dug into it a little bit. Your body probably ramps up, and your mind picks over the memory again. Notice this, as it happens, and practice your breathing.

And remember that habits are broken or changed by consistent actions in the direction you prefer. If you want to release the memory and allow it to process through, direct yourself to belly breathing when it arises, and remind yourself that the memory is about a past event. It no longer serves you to hold it. Decide to let it process and fall to the side.

Remember when I said "simple" was not the same as "easy"? Here is the perfect example. This is simple. But it isn't easy. It is, however, worthwhile and important on your journey of forgiving.

Your task in this step is not to forget the memories. It is to remove the energy from the memories and thoughts that have gotten too much energy and attention. Those memories won't be wiped from your mind. They will just lose their grip on you. What happened, happened. No debating that.

Since memories can keep us trapped, we want to loosen their grip. We want to remove the energy from those memories. It isn't so much about "healing" memories, as about putting memories where they need to be: thoughts about past events that are no longer happening and no longer threatening.

When memories emerge, remember it is just a thought — it is not happening and cannot hurt you. Nor does it need more energy from you. Decide you will release the thought, shift your energy away, and focus on belly breathing. Over time, the memory habit will subside. The memory will begin to lose energy — and will lose its power.

The next step is a learning process; we want to have a tool to deal with those memories. So, remember to practice the breathing.

STEP 4:
LEARN THE LESSONS

"**I** have nothing to learn," Anne told me, angry over my insinuation. "I have nothing to learn from an abusive man who abused a child."

There was silence. I could feel Anne's rage, now turned toward me.

But I pushed on. "Anne, I believe that every challenge and struggle instructs and guides us. Sometimes, we learn bad lessons. Sometimes, we learn good lessons. But the fact is, we learn from the events in our lives. Our task is to sort them into the lessons we want to hold and the lessons we need to release."

Anne stopped, looked up, and said, "Oh, I thought you meant lessons I learned from the abuse."

"Well, Anne, there *are* lessons you learned. For example, I know from your professional work that you have a special connection to children in difficult situations. You have a desire to protect the unprotected, to help people in similar situations. Is that right?"

She nodded.

I continued, "Your passion for that comes from lessons you learned from being defenseless. You have an understanding of that struggle that others do not. You have a clear purpose in defending those who can't do it themselves. That is a lesson."

Anne sat quietly.

"Sometimes, we learn lessons, but we don't even realize it. We forget what we have learned. This step is about learning the lessons," I explained. "Sometimes, we have to unlearn one lesson to learn another."

To be clear, I do not think that bad or hurtful things happen to people to teach them a lesson. It's actually from the other direction: when bad or hurtful things happen, we can learn from them. I don't think the universe is out to teach us a lesson, as much as we can (and do) learn lessons because of what happens to us.

Not all are good. Anne was suspicious and defensive with every man she met, deserved or not. Such unhelpful lessons have to be unlearned. Over time, Anne realized that some people are unsafe, but many others are kind and loving.

Some lessons are background parts of who we become. And other lessons need to be embraced. Anne's deep desire to protect the innocent and bring justice to those who hurt them is a part of who she is and needs to be embraced.

When "Will" came to see me, he shared his story of an overbearing bully of a father. Will's father controlled the family through his anger and threats of violence. At the slightest provocation, Will's father erupted in fits. He lashed out, breaking things and smacking family members.

While Will hated his childhood, he learned a lesson: you control others through anger and threats. While not the lesson one would want a child to learn, it is the one Will learned. At school, Will was the bully. Whenever he felt afraid, he lashed out in anger. And since Will was a fast grower, he ruled the playground.

Will took that same belief to college and became the frequent instigator of fights with rival fraternities. His friends stayed clear of his anger, many choosing to act friendly rather than risk the anger.

At every stage, this lesson was reinforced for Will. Will avoided his fear, got his way, and missed the fact that his "friends" lived in fear.

The bubble popped when Will married a woman far stronger than he gave credit. The first time Will erupted, she packed her bags and left, telling him it was time to "grow up and figure this out." She stated she would not return until Will "exorcised his demons."

And this is what brought Will into my office. With the exception of his father, Will had been able to use his anger to control everyone around him. It had worked for Will's father, and it had worked for Will.

Until it didn't.

Will loved his wife and was terrified of losing her. Unfortunately, that very fact was the reason for Will's violence. He had learned the lesson (not a good lesson) that he could use his anger to keep people from challenging him or leaving him. He just forgot that their feelings toward him were fear, not warmth or care.

As we talked, Will began to tell me about his family. We focused on his father. I asked him, "Will, did you love your father?"

Will looked up at me, "Love? I RESPECTED him. I knew that if I didn't, I would catch it. I respected him. What's love got to do with it?"

We sat in silence (a "therapeutic pause") while that processed. Then I opined, "Will, I think you confused fear and respect. I am not convinced you respected your father, but I am absolutely sure you feared him."

Another therapeutic pause.

"Maybe," Will whispered.

"But," I pushed, "it sounds to me like you want love. You want your wife to love you. You want friends to love you. Am I right?"

"Sure, I want to be loved. But I also want some respect. My wife just walked out. That's not respect."

"Will, that is self-respect. Your wife chose not to be another victim of your behavior, living in fear of you. I'm betting your wife would love to love you and respect you. But it sounds like she refuses to fear you."

For Will, he had learned a "lesson" from his childhood. It was just an unhelpful and unhealthy lesson of using fear to control, confusing fear with respect, and avoiding dealing with his own fear.

After a few sessions, Will began to realize his need to forgive his father. He had always seethed at his father, providing Will with a ready well of anger to foist on those around him. He started seeing the need to drain that well.

And Will began to learn a new lesson. In fact, he learned a few lessons, retrospectively, from those memories. He reflected upon the fear he felt for his father and realized he did not want to be feared. He recognized how his hurt had hurt others and worked to heal those hurts. Will also learned the tough lesson that his parents were human, flawed, and doing the best they could.

Will began to learn the lessons, both as a part of his forgiving and as a way to continue forgiving.

Sometimes, it is a matter of learning lessons, while unlearning other lessons. We are constantly learning. But we don't always get the lesson right. The Forgive Process usually includes righting the wrong lessons and learning the new ones.

This even flows into business situations, particularly where there are close relationships. Over the years, I have seen these patterns repeated in many family businesses and closely held companies.

I met "Bob" while consulting with his family business. The business and the family were falling apart. My task was to help the family members either to rescue the business or end it.

Bob's father started the company and built it into a sizable operation before handing it over to Bob and his siblings. All had enjoyed a comfortable life, the beneficiaries of the company's success. None of the family were particularly excited to work, much to the chagrin of the hard-working patriarch. But all liked the lifestyle the business provided. So, all worked in the company.

But, none saw the need to work hard. That included Bob, the appointed President. He turned over operations to others, popping in and out of the office. His "business luncheons," "business over golf," and "personal care" pretty much filled his calendar. And he left the fiscal oversight to a trusted friend.

That worked until checks began to bounce and the IRS came to the office. These events coincided with the sudden departure of Bob's CFO. After lots of hours with the accountants, it became clear that three paths had finally converged.

First, more and more hands were pulling at the profits as the family kept adding family employees. The business had served a single family well. But it was stretched to provide for five family units (and growing).

Second, the business was stagnating, if not contracting. Family members filled important positions but failed to bring energy or creativity into those positions. The momentum of the company slowed, costs went up, profit dropped.

Third, the "trusted friend" had been cooking the books and embezzling funds. In fact, the IRS was not getting the tax payments. After the family took their slices of the pie, the "friend" could only support his artificial lifestyle with a supplement from money owed to the IRS.

That was unsustainable. And the friend knew it. So, he had a plan. As the pieces began to fall in place, he vanished.

The day the IRS arrived, the friend did not show up for work — a first in twenty years. In retrospect, Bob realized that his friend was less "faithful" and more "keeping all tracks covered."

While other experts examined the viability for the company to continue, I worked with the family, helping them come together as a unit to support each other.

Bob was beside himself with anger. When I came into his office, he was pacing the floor. Accountants, agents, and attorneys were gathered around the imposing conference desk in his office.

Bob spent some time ranting, not really at me, but to whoever might listen. He raged about his "friend" and the betrayal. He raged about the workers who were "taking, taking, taking," but never giving back. He raged about the government "stealing us blind." And he raged about his family for "sucking the life from this company."

He never mentioned himself. His rage was toward others. I let that go for some time and finally suggested that perhaps we could walk and talk — away from his employees, family members, and federal agents.

On the walk, I asked Bob about the friend. Bob shared some choice descriptors with me. Then I asked, "But up until that day, who did you know him to be?" Bob stopped. His shoulders drooped. "He was my best friend from college," Bob shared. "I trusted him with everything. EVERYTHING!" Bob regained steam, quickly turning back to anger.

Over the next few weeks, the business hobbled along. The family members were tense with each other, and all were showing the stress of an unknown financial future. All the families were highly leveraged, having supported a lifestyle far above what even their once-profitable business could provide. All were suspect of each other, none were trusting the process. All were focused on doom, gloom, and destruction.

I spent time with Bob, helping him process the situation. His wound was deep. Bob realized he had not managed the business. One day, he brought in his calendar and showed me the pages. "This week, I think I worked five hours, and maybe eight that week. What was I thinking?"

I didn't answer.

Bob vacillated between personal consternation and angry tirades against the friend.

My task was helping the family system, but I understood what had happened in the business. "Bob, your friend contributed to where this business is. But he was not the only crumbling foundation. Your business environment changed, but you did not. Far too many hands were grabbing at a far too small pie. This was inevitable. Your friend simply sped it along."

Sometimes, a cold splash of reality helps. Sometimes, it turns out to be fuel for the fire. This time, it cooled Bob. It was time for lessons. So I asked Bob what lessons he took from this, going forward.

The first lesson was reactive, "You can't trust anyone."

I suggested Bob take a closer look. I suggested trust was a gift that needed to be carefully given and carefully guarded. But in the context of business, "trust" is better served through checks and balances — all completely absent from the business. So, I offered, "Bob, I don't think it was about trust, as much as avoidance. You didn't have any safeguards in place. Your friend could have been entirely trustworthy, and still been blamed. You would have had a hard time safeguarding him either way. You were trusting him because it was easier than doing the difficult stuff."

Bob was quieter now. "I suppose."

Through the next couple of hours, Bob realized there were some changes he needed to make in his own life. He realized that he actually did treasure the asset his father had built. He just didn't truly believe he had the skills to run it. So, he avoided it. Instead of learning the skills, he avoided the challenge. Bob realized that "blind trust" in business is a dangerous proposition. And Bob realized there had been no accountability anywhere in the business. All of the top people came and went as they pleased (mostly went). The rest of the company was adrift, left to figure out the path.

Over the next few weeks, Bob continued to learn the lessons. He noticed that the more he raged against his friend, the further he stood from the lessons. The more he recognized his role and responsibility, the more his anger eased. Yes, his friend betrayed him. Yes, it was wrong, unethical, and illegal. Yes, his friend should be held responsible. But in this case, the family — and Bob in particular — created an environment where it could go undetected for years and years.

Every event teaches lessons. In fact, the most memorable lessons come from the most memorable events. We collect information and understanding throughout life. But those events tend to collate and organize the information, turning them into lessons.

These lessons can be unexamined realities. This step is to process the lessons, learn the ones that are worthwhile and discard the ones that don't serve you (and are likely not entirely accurate).

CLARITY POINT: To restate, I do not believe something happens in order for you to learn a lesson. I don't believe the universe conspires against you in order to bring you grief and pain.

I do believe there is something to be learned from difficult events and relationships. Those lessons may keep us from stepping into the path of the same type of event or people. Those lessons may make us more compassionate toward others in difficult situations. Those lessons may help us understand ourselves and others more deeply.

CONSIDER THESE QUESTIONS:

1. What lessons did I learn from this person/event? Are they lessons I want to hold onto? Do they serve me or hinder me?

2. How did this event/person shape my view of the universe, the world, people, relationships, and myself? Do those lessons serve me or hinder me?

3. Who have I become as a result of those experiences? Is that who I want to be and need to be?

4. How has this experience shaped my role in my own life? Does it hold me back or move me forward?

Every experience and situation, good or bad, teaches us lessons. Some are lessons to be learned, and some are lessons to be unlearned. In this process of forgiving, you have already been through the experience. At least make it helpful, either by the lesson you learn or the lesson you unlearn in the process of forgiving.

Lessons usually expand over time. Right now, you are working to nurture a habit of looking for the lessons. If you think there are none, keep looking. If you find a small lesson, it will likely expand. If you find some pretty big lessons, let them filter through and consolidate. But keep looking for the lessons.

As part of that process, you will now want to turn your attention to, not the person or event involved, but you. Remember that through life, you always take yourself. Many times, when we are hurt and hurting, we tend to become self-focused and yet look outward.

It is easy to become self-focused, forgetting that the rest of the world struggles through life. This self-focus is the starting point of getting caught in "victim-mode." This is neither productive nor healthy.

Learning the lessons helps to shift us to a productive self-examination. Which leads to examining the roles played in life.

STEP 5:
ACCEPT YOUR ROLE
(AND CHOOSE YOUR ROLE)

This next step is tough for many people. They see the title of the step and assume they are now being blamed for what happened. If that was your visceral response, hear me out. (You **may** be right, but give me a chance.)

Shakespeare wrote that "All the world's a stage, and all the men and women merely players." Which points to the fact that as the drama of life unfolds, we all play various roles. Think about it: who you are with one group of friends is different than who you are with another group. How you act with friends is likely different than how you act with parents and other family members, or coworkers on the job. Most of us play different roles.

There is also a deeper level than this: we aren't operating on a completed script. We are making the script up as we go — as are others around us. We keep re-writing our character, our role in the drama.

And there is yet a deeper level: how we play a certain role **often** determines some of how that scene plays out. I say "often," because there are times when, no matter what we do, the outcome is based on the circumstances already in play.

Sometimes, we do everything "right," only to find ourselves at the wrong place at the wrong time. We might just be caught in circumstances beyond our control.

As I write this book, our world is caught in a refugee crisis. Many of those refugees were simply doing what you and I are doing: going through life, doing the best we can.

When war or disaster strikes, daily life is upended through no fault (no causation) of the person who then becomes a refugee. Often, the act of becoming a refugee is an attempt to make a bad situation better. The situation was not caused by the person. It acted upon the person, leading to consequences for the person.

Let's consider roles in three parts: the role you played before, the role you played during, and the role you play after that situation which brings you to this book. And let's clearly differentiate "role" with "fault." It is impossible to NOT play a role in any situation. There may be some choices in the role played. But it is impossible to not have a role in a situation in which you find yourself.

We can't re-write the role of who you were, but you can choose the role you play from here. And that gets to the heart of this step: Accept Your Role (and Choose Your Role). "Who were you?" That is one question. "Who will you be?" That is another question (and far more important).

Throughout life, we try on life lessons, accept or discard them, and reshape our own self-identity. The process can push us toward "survival mode" or "thrival mode." One is about just getting by, often feeling like a victim. The other is about thriving, choosing a path of *responsible*.

CLARITY POINT: "Responsible" is far different than "fault." Our culture tends to confuse the two. Fault is about blame, finding someone to point the finger at. It is always about looking back to see who can be blamed — usually in an attempt to ameliorate personal fault. If I can find someone else to blame or fault, I can walk away feeling innocent. Which tends to be a fairly binary decision: at fault/not at fault. No shared responsibility. It is only about who, in particular, can hold the blame.

Responsibility is a bit different. It is all about being "Response-Able." You have the ability to respond in different ways. Fault points backward, into the past. Responsible points from now into the future. It is about a choice in actions and thoughts, from this point forward, as a way of making life different.

While many people use the words as synonyms ("Who's at fault/responsible?"), let me suggest you distinguish between blame and choice. If you are in a burning building, it is a waste of time to ask, "Who started this fire? Who did this? (Who shall we blame?)" It is much more powerful and helpful to ask, "What do I need to do to get myself and my loved ones out of here?" That is the question of response, of choosing responsible.

Which brings us back to roles. Examining the roles played gives us the opportunity of choosing the next roles.

"Casey" was at one of my seminars. I can remember it so clearly because it was one of those moments I thought the participants were about to turn on me. Casey rescued me in her clarity.

We were naming the "unforgivables," as I sought to make the point that "unforgivable" comes from misunderstanding the concept of forgiveness (see the earlier section, "Myths of Forgiveness"). One person in the group named as an unforgivable, "men hurting women or children." I wrote it on the whiteboard and asked for clarification. This person explained that there was no excuse for a man to be violent or hurtful to a woman or child. It was, she said, "unacceptable and inexcusable. You can't forgive that one."

As I was beginning to turn this around and talk about the fact that everything is forgivable, since it frees up the one who forgives and not the forgiven, the chilly shift in the atmosphere was a bit unnerving. The room was in agreement, and I was about to try to make a lesson out of this. I swallowed hard.

Then Casey spoke. "My ex-husband is in jail now. He was busted for drugs. But also domestic violence. He beat me, and my kids, on many occasions." The room's energy shifted to Casey. People were immediately supportive and sympathetic for her. The woman who volunteered this "unforgivable" even turned to me and said, "See?"

Then Casey spoke again. "No, you are wrong. That is not unforgivable. I am realizing I have to forgive so I can move forward. I can't live trapped by that. I can't stay the victim. And if I can't forgive, I am stuck."

The other woman responded, "But this isn't your fault. It is all on him. He has to be held 100% at fault. He needs to be in jail. You don't need to do anything."

Casey responded, "Yes, I do. I am here because I don't want to be defined by that relationship. And I have been defining myself in ways that are not healthy. He isn't the first abusive relationship I have been in. I need to figure out why I keep finding people who would hurt me."

The woman tried to defend Casey to herself, "But those men are the ones at fault. You are the victim."

Through tears, Casey responded, "I kept putting myself in those situations. Yes, he does need to be in jail for his actions. But I can't just pretend I was a pawn. I knew he had problems and I still moved in with him. I knew about the drugs and that he had been violent, and I still chose to move in. In fact, I moved in because of the drugs. But more than that, I stayed. I put up with insults. Then yelling. I stayed. Then throwing things. Then pushing me. I stayed. And then hitting me. I stayed. I have to recognize I played a role. I am not at fault for his actions. But I had a role in what happened to me."

The room sat silent. I stood silent. We were all amazed at Casey's vulnerability and awareness. Fault-finding is an easy way to avoid both forgiving and changing. Casey wanted to make a change. She wanted to forgive. And she also was willing to examine her role in her life — not just her role in that relationship, but her role in her entire life.

But notice what Casey was not saying. She did not say she made her ex-husband hit her or abuse her. She did not claim a role in causing the abuse. But she was willing to think about her role in even being in that situation. These are very different things. Casey did not make or cause her ex-husband to abuse. But she was clear that she chose a path that kept her in a potentially dangerous situation.

When we are hurt and angry (really, the same thing), we often want to look for fault. We want to find someone (or something) ultimately at fault and to blame. Our next step is to de-humanize and then demonize that person. Ironically, this often leaves us once again stuck, the victim of a situation in which we feel no choice or control.

Once we accept our role, we are free to change it and choose a different one. Casey believed herself to be the victim. Since she had been in abusive relationships before, she just decided she was destined to be hurt, to be in abusive relationships. The role Casey played kept her stuck — until she decided to stop playing that role.

As Casey proclaimed to the group, "Don't see me as the victim. I did that for years. And for years I have been stuck in one bad relationship after another. I will not go back to that."

We all have choices and responsibilities for relationships we enter into and remain within. Sometimes, it is a matter of luck — the family we are born into or the person(s) we bump into. The question is then about our choices to stay or leave the relationships in our lives.

We also are responsible for the choices we make in life that lead, like falling dominoes, to other events. Sometimes, the dominoes fall toward good things. Sometimes, they fall toward bad, hurtful, or painful things.

While a chaplain, I spent hours with people given horrible diagnoses. I covered the oncology floor, many people being repeat patients. They came in for treatment on a regular basis. But it was also ground zero for a terminal diagnosis. That meant that I was often interacting with people from the point of a terminal diagnosis to the end of life.

I noticed that people tended to branch into two distinct groups, not based on diagnosis, but on reaction to the diagnosis. Some became bitter and angry about the "cards dealt to them." Others were interested in how to play out those cards. They weren't happy about the diagnosis. But they knew that in arguing and fighting against it, they simply gave all their energy to the disease and not to living.

This had nothing to do with treatment choices or hopes in beating cancer. It was more a matter of relationship to the cancer. Many found themselves unfairly struck by the illness. Others simply saw themselves as having to deal with the diagnosis.

Let me be clear: role is not about causation — although there *may* be a layer to that. It is about identity in the face of a situation. It is watching how you play out situations.

Late one evening, I was called to the oncology floor. Generally, that meant a patient either had a theological question or was struggling emotionally. Staff ran lower through those hours, and family had gone home. I was often the one called upon to spend some time with particular patients.

The nurse at the station pointed me to the room requesting a chaplain. As I gently knocked and opened the door to the room, it was mostly dark. A small light was on, and the medical instruments let off a glow. As did the end of the lit cigarette. (This was in the days when patients were still allowed to smoke in their rooms — even while breathing pure oxygen!)

I announced myself and approached the bedside. I asked, "I understand you requested a chaplain; can I sit with you?" I think I saw a nod. I took it as such and sat down beside the bed.

My new friend stared at the ceiling, continuing to puff his cigarette. Finally, he spoke, "Chaplain, I have lung cancer. I'm dying." This was a recent diagnosis, made during the last day. I knew this from the nurse. He was terminal.

"Why did God do this to me?" he asked, "Why did God give me cancer?"

I paused. Then asked, "Before I try to answer that, can I ask you a question?"

He nodded.

So I ventured, "How long have you been smoking?"

My friend shared that he started smoking in his early teens. It started with his friends, sneaking a smoke. It was a habit he never broke, smoking up to a couple of packs a day for years. Then, he coughed up some blood. He had noticed his cough, but there had been a cough for years. Suddenly, there was blood along with the cough. That led him to the doctor, and finally to this moment.

I pushed a bit, "Do you think, maybe, that had some effect? Perhaps part of the issue is not about God causing the cancer, but that smoking may have contributed?"

It was a silent moment. Then he nodded. After a pause, he asked, "So, you think this is my fault?"

I suggested, "I'm not sure that 'fault' is a particularly useful discussion. You want to blame because you are scared. I just wanted to clarify that there are plenty of factors that might lead to this. The real question, though, is what you do from here."

He turned, looked at me, and said, "Chaplain, there ain't nothing I can do. I am going to die."

I hoped we had established enough of a relationship for my friend to hear me. I offered, "I am not really thinking about how to beat this. I am thinking more about how to live until you die. Are there people you want to see? Things you need to do? Conversations you need to have? You have time. Looking for who to blame is probably not part of what you want to do during the rest of your time."

We sat silently. He stared at the ceiling.

Then he turned and said, "You're right. I don't have much time. But I do have some things I need to say."

I was not looking for my friend's role in causing the cancer. That was long in the rear-view mirror. The more important role was how he lived out the rest of his days. Questions of fault were unlikely to serve him well in his final days.

Often, we need to clarify the roles we played and the roles we want to play. Seeing where we have been can help us decide upon where we want to go. Not by the forces around us, but by our choices. It is how we deliberately and consciously move forward.

The roles we play shift over time. So, in the Forgive Process, let's consider your role from several different timeframes.

In terms of the incident or incidents that bring you to this Process, consider these three points of your role: *before*, *during*, and *after*.

For some, little will be gained from examining the "before" role. For others, this role is critical to understand.

Anne, who suffered abuse at the hands of her father, will not learn much. She was a child born into a threatening and abusive situation. She did not play a role in what caused the abuse. The issues with her father were there long before Anne was born. She was just another target, having little choice in being there.

Bob, however, whose family business was destroyed, played an important role. Since Bob was not doing his job, the business was vulnerable. Bob needed to examine his role as a way of understanding why he was in this mess. Yes, he was a victim of a crime. AND part of how that crime could happen was because of the role Bob played (or failed to play).

> *CLARITY POINT: Again, this step is not about blame or fault. It is, though, a very important assessment of personal responsibility. This is not about "blaming the victim," as much as taking responsibility, both for what was happening and what happens. If Bob cannot see his role, he cannot change it for the*

> *next time. For Anne, it was important for her to see there was nothing she, as a small child, could have done to prevent this.*
>
> *Interestingly, many people minimize their role, while others magnify their role. Both miss some understandings that can be transformational to their lives. We can accept too little power or too much power in situations over which we had control or didn't have control.*

At first, Bob reacted at my pushing him to look at his culpability. He did not want to be seen as having any responsibility. But as we examined his role, Bob was able to make a shift to accept his role.

At first, Anne reacted at my pushing her to look at her innocence. She had always believed, deep down inside, that perhaps she could have prevented her father's anger. If she had been quieter, more careful (more anything), maybe he wouldn't have been so angry. But as we examined her role, Anne was able to make a shift, seeing that her role had little to do with her father's abuse.

Casey worked to claim an appropriate role. She had been involved in the drug use (which was why she was in her ex-husband's vicinity). She knew about his temper. She put herself in a dangerous predicament. And she stayed, even as it grew more violent. Was Casey responsible for her ex-husband's behavior? Not in any way. Was Casey responsible for being in the vicinity, the sphere of danger? Yes. And Casey worked to make sure that would never be true again.

As was true for Casey, the other important role is the role you assume after an incident/incidents. Do you continue to allow that event(s) to define who you are and how you interact with the world? If so, is that appropriate or reactive?

Sometimes, people assume the role of victim. Not just an awareness of having been victimized, but of having played the role of victim. This leads to disempowerment and helplessness. It creates a "stuckness" that is hard to escape. And involuntarily, it tends to set people up for further victimization.

Funny thing about roles: we take them on because they "work." At least, they seem to work for a time. We hold onto the roles because they "worked." There is only one problem: many roles we play really only serve to hold us back. They tie us to events where we played that role (and where the role may have even been helpful).

Roles are like habits. When we form them, they serve a purpose. The problem is that even after the purpose no longer works, we often keep playing that role.

Just to be clear, I don't in any way believe that those roles are consciously chosen. We fall into roles because they worked (at one time). We get stuck in roles because they become habit. But we can always choose a different role. While earlier roles may have been unconsciously chosen, new roles can be consciously chosen.

Consider the role you played before the incident. Was it more like Anne or more like Bob? Was your role just a fact of where you were born? Or was it more like Bob, where your role set up some unfortunate circumstances?

Consider the role you played during the incident. Were you more like Anne, just trying to survive? Or more like Casey, not sure how to change to get away? Or more like Bob, participating in the continuing actions?

Your purpose, again, is not so you can blame yourself. It is to see the role so you can choose a different role. Who do you want to be in life? How do you want to choose a different path?

Remember that, like actors discover moving from movie to movie, you can always assume a new role. The core YOU will be there, but the role you play can shift. You get to choose that role when you decide you can. And different roles take us to different places in life. Choose your role to follow a different script.

Which brings us to the final piece of this process, looping us around to the beginning. You started with a decision, and you "end" the process with a decision.

STEP 6:
RE-DECIDE AND REINFORCE

To *decide* is to "cut off" or "kill off," coming from a Latin word, *decidere*. It is not simply making a choice. When you decide, you cut off all other options. When you *decide* to do something, it is a choice to move in that direction, cutting off all other options.

When you decide to forgive, you are choosing that path, leaving behind the options of not forgiving — and of being bound to an event, incident, or person. And at the end of the Forgive Process, it is a matter of re-deciding and reinforcing that choice. In fact, that is the last step of the process.

In the first step, you decided to forgive. That was without an awareness of the process to actually get there. You stepped forward in a choice to forgive. Perhaps it just felt like it was time to do it. Or perhaps you made that choice, kicking and screaming. Still, you made the decision and have moved through the intervening four steps between deciding and here.

We now arrive at the end of the process, only to find that the process continues. You've done the work of the other steps.

Now, you recommit to your decision and continue to reinforce that choice.

Why is this a necessary step?

Because humans tend to cycle our thoughts. As we discussed early on, forgiving is not the same as forgetting. At this point, you may remember from a different perspective. You may have a deeper view of yourself, the incident(s), and the person. But that does not erase the memories.

Remnants will take a while to "settle out." If you grab a scoop of river water, you might notice lots of "stuff" from the agitation. It gets stirred up. Everything seems to be everywhere. Given a little time and gravity, the "stuff" settles to the bottom, and you can scoop out the clear water from the top.

Sometimes, the stuff in our psyche gets agitated and swirls around. If you were struggling with something (not forgiving, but struggling), it stays agitated. In the process of forgiving, the stuff might seem even more agitated. But the forgiving stills the waters and the lets the stuff start to settle out.

That doesn't mean the stuff isn't there. The memories and thoughts are still down there, waiting for a stir. And life tends to stir every now and then. Don't be surprised when a thought or memory catches you and hurts. You may even ask, "Did I really forgive?" And if you share the thought with someone, they may say, "I thought you had forgiven." You did; this is normal.

Don't allow the remnants to pull you back. It is the nature of memories for them to be triggered (usually, though, at a decreasing rate). And it is the nature of your brain to still want to warn you. That does not mean you have not forgiven. It simply means the process continues.

"Kelly" wanted desperately to forgive her former best friend. They were partners in a small boutique together. Kelly was the more sensible "feet on the floor," while her partner was "head in the sky." Both shared an impeccable taste in fashion and decor.

When they opened their little shop, it was instantly busy. They were caught a bit off-guard and had to scramble to keep up and stay stocked. Both were at the shop way too much. They were almost the victims of their own success.

Once things leveled out, Kelly and her partner breathed — and then started disagreeing. Kelly was pleased with their success but chalked it up to a good location and good merchandise. Kelly's partner was sure that she, herself, was the "magic sauce." Her partner started making choices without talking with Kelly.

As their partnership deteriorated, attorneys stepped in. Kelly refused to relinquish her part of the partnership regardless of her partner's continued efforts to eliminate Kelly. Her partner remained convinced that any and all success was because of her own efforts, with Kelly only functioning as "hired help."

Legal fees crunched the store's reserves. Kelly couldn't sleep and slipped into depression. Her partner stopped coming to work but continued making decisions from home. They finally worked out a dissolution of the partnership.

Kelly had dreamed of this shop since childhood, and she was watching it grind toward bankruptcy. In the end, Kelly was left with the shop, its lease, and the remaining inventory. In return, Kelly handed a check over to her ex-partner. Her ex-partner opened a rival shop just across the street and a few doors down. Kelly was stuck with debt, worse off than if she had simply opened a new shop herself. And every day, Kelly had to come to work and see both shops.

It was a daily reminder for Kelly. She kept re-living the arguments, the feelings of desperation, the broken trust.

Even after we worked through the Forgive Process together — even as Kelly became clear of her own role in the process, even as she began to see her ex-partner from a more human perspective, and even as she learned some important lessons — Kelly came face to face with her pain every day. It was, literally, right across the street.

She had to re-decide to forgive. Daily. Her ex-partner continued to talk badly about Kelly, spreading misinformation and lies to customers and vendors. Kelly continued to choose forgiveness.

It took time and effort, but Kelly realized one day that she had birthed the business she had always wanted, then raised it through a difficult adolescence. When she walked into her shop every morning, she realized she had actually built her childhood dream. She refused to give up her dream to someone else.

And over time, vendors experienced the difference between Kelly's shop and her ex-partner's shop. Kelly followed through, paid her invoices on time, and didn't change her orders on a daily basis. And she didn't blame the vendors when customers didn't quickly purchase everything. Kelly began to have more and more exclusive deals with vendors.

Kelly realized that by going through the Forgive Process,

she wasn't sabotaging herself. She wasn't reacting because she chose to forgive; not in an instant, but over time.

How do you re-decide and recommit? When a memory pops up, you remind yourself that you are forgiving. Look to see if there is anything new or helpful in that memory. Does it broaden your understanding of yourself, the person(s), or the event(s)? If so, take that in and add it to your process. If not, disengage from the memory.

How do you disengage from the memory? By belly breathing and reminding yourself that it is not happening right now, it is simply a thought. And you can choose whether you give that thought energy or release it. And breathe.

It might not work the first time (and maybe not the second or third time) because of thought habits. We tend to have a habit of taking thoughts and turning them over. We are used to giving the thought/memory energy and attention. It is habitual. So, we have to do some re-training to break the pattern.

When you are stuck in a thought habit, remind yourself of the lessons you learned from what happened, accept that you can't change it, move through the memory, and remind yourself that you still choose to forgive.

Many people want forgiveness to be instantaneous, and immediate. It would be nice if we could simply decide to forgive someone and have everything fall into place. Rarely is that the case for anything significant or important. In fact, most people discover that forgiving people for big transgressions is a process. If you can forgive and let it go easily, it probably was not one of the bigger life events.

If a friend makes a cross comment, you might let it go in an instant or maybe even a couple of days. But if a friend truly betrays you, the process can take some time. Still, it can happen. If a stranger harms you, the process can take some time. Still, it can happen. If a family member hurts or betrays you, the process can take some time. Still, it can happen. An event can pull you back into the hurt and pain, the betrayal and disappointment. This is why you re-decide to forgive and reinforce the decision to move forward.

Oh, and this is not a linear process — it is a zig-zagging process. Once you decide to forgive, you may cycle through empathizing, breathing, examining, lesson-learning, and bouncing back and forth between them. Many people find that as they are looking for roles and lessons, they have to repeatedly breathe through the memories that stir. Sometimes, looking for the lesson shows the roles. Sometimes, roles include lessons. And new perspectives emerge through those roles and lessons, which tends to create new levels of empathy.

Don't think of the steps as completely distinct. They cross back and forth into each other. As you are building empathy, you may find a lesson. As you examine your role, you may build empathy. The steps are just the next places of intentionality, not separations from the other steps.

Let the steps be a framework. But don't let them be part of being stuck. They flow together and cross paths throughout the journey. The important thing, though, is to be on the journey.

At this point, you have decided to not be a prisoner of an event or another person's actions. Stay that course. Progress is progress. If it is slower than you wish, it is still progress. There are times when the process might feel slow. And there are times when a step simply falls into place.

When I have time, I love to trail run. Part of the trail experience is dealing with ever-varying terrain. Sometimes, I am flying down a hill, letting gravity pull me. Other times, I am pushing up a hill, fighting that same gravity. My speed can vary wildly. And then there are times when I am picking my way through obstacles — a scree field, downed trees, streams — that slow me down due to the need to pay such close attention.

Unlike running on a road, where you might be able to hold a steady state and pace, the trail can vary wildly on speed. I don't worry about my pace, I just stay focused on making progress. One step at a time. Fast in spots, slow in others, and careful in others. But I still make progress, even if it requires a breather here or there.

Re-decide to forgive. Let the steps solidify. And remember: this is a process — circular at times, painful at points, frustrating and freeing. Just when you feel like you aren't making progress, you break through. It requires a re-decision, a commitment.

Stick with it.

You are reclaiming your power and your life. You are deciding that no event or person gets to control your thoughts, your emotions, or your life. Forgiving is reclaiming what has been captured and held from you. It is finding freedom to live. Not *because* of what has happened. Not *in spite* of what has happened. But *regardless* of what has happened.

Your life is your choice, once you accept that. Choose to forgive and release what holds you back. One step at a time. But ever moving toward your choice to reclaim your life for yourself.

Ready for the journey? It starts now.

Q & A on Forgiving

As people move through this process, similar questions emerge. Let me try to answer the most common questions I hear from people on a regular basis as they move through the process.

"I can't seem to make it to the last step. I keep going back and forth. Why can't I follow the steps?"

While I lay out the process in a step-by-step fashion, that doesn't mean you will proceed linearly, from 1 to 2 to 3 to 4 to 5 to 6. While it is hard to move on to the next step as you are still working through one step, that doesn't mean you won't bounce between the steps. The first step and the last step mark points on the journey.

You can't start the journey until you take step 1. And generally, I find each step follows the next. But you may not have finished a step before finding yourself returning to a previous step. For instance, you may learn lessons, then examine your role, only to discover new lessons to be learned. You may be in the process of looking at your role, only to be overwhelmed with thoughts. All you can do then is breathe and wait for the memory to release.

The steps are part of a process — more like a winding trail than a staircase. You may think, "Haven't I been here before?" Maybe. Or perhaps it is just a similar place to move through.

The steps provide a framework, a way to think through the process. But they are far less divided than the framework would indicate. They tend to blur into each other at times. Consider it a process and keep moving.

"You can't make me forgive. I won't do it."

You are correct. I cannot make you forgive. And I certainly am not here to make you forgive. Consider it an invitation. IF you want to forgive, these are the steps you can take. But you don't have to.

However, notice the power you give up when you choose NOT to forgive. You may think you are holding onto power. But actually, you are giving events and people emotional power in your life. You may want to reclaim that power.

The energy given to other people and events does not serve your life. It keeps you from living fully. And it requires a decision. I invite you to forgive. But I can't insist.

"How dare you tell me I played a role! This was done TO me. I didn't deserve or want it. Why do you think I played a role?"

Roles are funny things. It's not always about choosing; sometimes you are thrown into a role, and you can't escape it. We all have a role, but roles are not about fault.

Remember that the examination of a role is not the assignment of blame. There are many times when we are victims of an event. And there are times when we get stuck in the role of victim.

There are also times when we contributed to the lead-up to an event, or even to the event itself. Those are painful examinations.

Looking for your role is not the same as blaming yourself. It is simply looking at the role you played before, during, and after. Playing a role is unavoidable.

I've noticed that many times, people play a role and refuse to accept it. And other times, I've seen people blame themselves for a role they didn't even have — because they really were the victims. Which then raises the more important question about "what's next?" What role do you choose in moving forward, apart from the event(s)?

Really, the most important role is the role you choose in moving forward, with who you want to be and how you want to interact with the world. Examining the role only allows you room to choose the role you now want.

"You said we all have a role in any situation we are in. Well, I had no role. I was just in the car hit by the drunk driver (or substitute any situation in which you were "just there"). No role. Right?"

Let's be clear: If you were there, you had a role. But that is not the same as you "sharing blame/fault/responsibility." I was sitting at a stoplight when an inattentive driver plowed into the back of my almost-new vehicle. It was not my fault; I was stopped at a red light. But in the actions of that event, I was there, and my role was simply as driver of the car in the way of his vehicle. I don't have to feel like I made a mistake or caused it. The accident was all on him.

But what happens next is up to me. I was fortunate. We were largely uninjured, and really only had to deal with getting the car repaired once everyone agreed to fault. I didn't choose any legal process after the accident since the car was repaired. But I could have posed this as a "Why does this always happen to me?" frame that sets me up as a victim of life. I could have continued with that role indefinitely. At that point, I would have assumed another role, one that was unnecessary and unhelpful.

To stick with that metaphor, though, there are times when a car accident is caused by the actions of both people. Both contributed to the accident. Perhaps one was in the role of inattentive driver, the other in the role of intoxicated driver or even angry driver. Both roles contribute to the accident.

A couple of years ago, I watched an accident unfold as two drivers, both looking at their cell phones, tried to change lanes at the same time. I saw both were looking down. It was not a major accident, but the cars were jammed together, trying to merge into a lane.

The police arrived, and I watched as one person said, "I was looking at my phone." The other proclaimed, "I had nothing to do with this! It was the other driver!" With three witnesses corroborating the reality of two drivers looking down, the role chosen by the second driver didn't last long. He had to accept his role of partial fault.

The step is to examine the role you were playing before the event, the role you were playing during the event, and the role you play after the event. *Sometimes*, you will find you hold responsibility for what led up to the event. *Sometimes*, you realize you contributed during the event. And *sometimes*, you realize the role you play after the event is counter-productive. This step around looking at roles is just about examining the roles, to see the role(s) you did play.

Again, this is not to assign blame to yourself. It is to examine your roles to see if you want to step into a new role.

Sometimes, people find themselves playing the role of victim, and yet they have some responsibility in their role. Sometimes, people blame themselves, and yet they were truly the victim. This step is simply an examination of roles.

Having a role in any situation in which you are involved is unavoidable. But having a role isn't about blame or fault; it isn't about causation. It is a matter of presence. Being there means you had a role.

That said, we all do get to choose the role we wish to play, starting here and now, moving forward. Examining the roles is simply assuming a choice on the role moving forward. You can't change the role you played. You don't need to. But this process is an opportunity to choose a role moving forward.

(NOTE: "Choosing a role" is not necessarily changing your role. You may be clear that the role you are playing is the role you want to play. But at that point, you make it a conscious choice.)

"Lessons? Why should I learn a lesson? This shouldn't have happened. That is the lesson."

Maybe that *is* the lesson. But broaden it out a bit. Things like this shouldn't happen; that is the basic lesson. So, is there something that can be changed? Either to keep it from happening to others or to help others when it happens?

There is also something deeper. Every event, every interaction has the potential to teach. We just have to be looking for the lesson.

And you DID learn a lesson (or lessons). The question is whether you can un-learn the harmful lessons and embrace the helpful ones.

Humans are, at our core, learners. We are naturally curious, and constantly trying to find better ways to move forward. When that is not happening, it is pretty clear evidence of being stuck. The question becomes, "What is keeping me stuck?"

Sometimes, it is a lesson waiting to be learned. When we don't learn the lesson, it tends to keep popping up in our lives, waiting for the next opportunity. It is part of our development to get to a place where we must either learn the lesson or remain stuck. That lesson tends to wait us out.

We often keep stumbling over it until we finally examine it. That is the nature of those life lessons. It is a question of either learning them or being stuck until we do — since the lesson is usually what allows us to move forward.

So, I am suggesting that you look for any lessons to be learned. First, it is good for growth. And second, it frees you to continue moving forward.

You can't help but learn lessons. They will wait for you. It is not a "should" when it comes to learning; it is just how we are built. We will learn. The question is when.

"This is too hard. Why should I have to dig up the painful memories?"

Those painful memories are already there. I'm not suggesting you dig them up — you don't have to because they are already there. In fact, I am suggesting you breathe through those memories and release them.

My goal is to help you move through the memory.

In my experience, most people *want* to stop re-living the memories, but don't know how. So, they try to shove them aside and ignore them. Instead of resolving and releasing, those memories just keep waiting. They don't go anywhere, mostly because they are still given space in your mind — even if it is only a holding space, just off to the side, but never far from awareness.

"If those memories are there, shouldn't they be there?"

This question is more a way to rationalize holding onto those memories. Yes, the memories are there, and yes, they might just stay. Over time, though, they may do less and less damage. They become a fact of life, not constant torments.

The question of "shouldn't they be there" is kind of like saying, "Our house is a mess with stuff all around. But it's there, so I guess the mess should be there." An accumulation of anything is not justification for it staying around, as much as it is a statement of accumulation.

There are orienting events in all of our lives. These pivotal moments are defining experiences. The question is whether the pivotal moments bring us to a more thriving life or keep us just surviving. Remember, it is not a matter of "doing this right," but rather deciding to move through an experience.

A number of years ago, I was speaking with a family. The adult twin women were trying to iron out some disagreements and hurts from over the years. Both noted an orienting event in their lives: the death of their mother when they were 15 years old. Their mother died of cancer after a long battle that covered the developmental years from age 10 to 15 for these girls (now women).

Both had been through the same event. One was angry and bitter with God, constantly railing against an "unfair universe and mean God." She was angry at her mother for leaving, her father for grieving, and her sister for moving on.

The other sister said she would always miss having her mother around for big life events, but also told me she knew her mother wanted to be there, too. She had long forgiven God, realizing that everyone dies, and the only question is how and when.

After watching the medical world for those five years, this sister became a doctor, specializing in oncology — the treatment of cancer.

I am not saying that one way was right and the other was wrong. I am simply noting that both had been through the same orienting event. One took that event and moved toward a thriving life (even though she, too, had to rebuild her life after such a loss). The other took the event as a blow that knocked her down and kept her down. She could not release it, and had a list of "unforgivens." She held God, her father, her mother, her sister, and the medical community responsible. As she told painful memory after painful memory, she was using the memories as a way to remind herself of why those people deserved blame — to continually rebuild her case against those whom she deemed unforgivable.

Her sister shared the same memories. She used them as points of empathy when working with her patients. And it kept her focused on helping people to survive their illness.

Those memories anchored one to pain and provided motivation to the other.

The memories are not going anywhere. The real question is whether the memories serve your growth or trap you. Part of that depends upon the energy devoted to remembering, versus allowing the memories to be.

"Why should I forgive someone? They need to be held responsible. They need to pay a price. You just want me to let them off the hook? That seems unfair."

Why should you continue to pay the price for something that has already happened? Why should you be held captive by the actions of someone else? Those are the reasons I suggest you forgive.

If you think you are holding the offender responsible, there are two possibilities.

First, you could be wrong. They may not even be aware of the harm caused, may not feel responsible, and may no longer even be around.

Second, they may already be paying a price. You gain nothing from trying to extract more. If they are already being held accountable and responsible, does it serve you to mete out more punishment? Can you leave that to others?

"What about justice?"

Justice is independent of forgiveness. It rarely comes from the person who is hurt; it is often external. Often, it comes from authority, someone able to mete out the penalty for an offense.

If the person who hurt you broke the law, it becomes a legal issue for the courts. Turn it over to them, if necessary, and let them do their job.

That does not prevent you from moving through the forgiving process, though. If it does, you are stuck waiting for justice to come. And it can be a long wait, indeed.

Often, when we are hung up on justice, the real issue lurking behind it is fairness. We want something that will even it all out. The "eye for an eye, tooth for a tooth" level of justice is really about revenge and evening things out. It is based on "being fair." If someone took a certain amount, they must pay that same amount, at their own loss.

Revenge does little for "fairness" or even justice. You can't replace your pain by causing another to be in pain. This only keeps you wrapped up in reaction and hurt. And it doesn't truly shift anything. Instead of releasing, it tends to trap.

For this process, turn the question of justice over to the authority who can mete it out, and work to release — discovering that you are mostly releasing yourself.

"It's too late. The person who hurt me is dead/gone/ absent. There's nothing I can do. Right?"

Wrong.

Remember, forgiving someone may have nothing to do with re-establishing a relationship. If fact, the person may not even be aware of you forgiving them. So, they don't have to be present and don't even have to be alive. It just requires you to decide to forgive.

Notice that there are no steps in the Forgive Process that require the other person to be present or have knowledge. Only a decision by you to not be held by the events any longer.

Many people wait for someone to ask for forgiveness before they apologize. They reason that forgiving starts there. Which only places the power with the person you want to apologize. If they don't or can't apologize, it keeps you stuck.

If you find yourself stuck in this equation, "IF they apologize, THEN I will forgive," let me suggest another one which places the power and choice with you: "I will forgive, REGARDLESS of whether the other person apologizes or acknowledges."

Waiting leaves you stuck. Choosing to forgive, regardless of another's actions (or lack of action), restores your choice and power.

"It just seems so unfair that I have to be the one to forgive, since I was wronged. I think the person should be begging for forgiveness. It just seems so weak to forgive."

Sometimes, our cultural habits catch us. This is really about the difference between "having" to forgive and "getting" to forgive. It is the difference between *forgiving for the other person*, versus *forgiving for yourself.*

When you forgive, you are not weak. You are assuming your own power. You are choosing to no longer be held hostage by an event. Instead, you are stepping forward and deciding you will not be trapped by another's actions.

That takes power, responsibility, acceptance, and a decision to move forward. There is nothing weak about that.

If you are forced to wait for another person's actions in order to be free from something, that is a truly weak position. Power comes from assuming responsibility for your choices and actions. Power comes from disconnecting from the actions/ inactions of another person.

Forgiveness comes from power, not weakness. Choose to forgive, so that YOU are released from the actions of another.

"I always think about the fact that if I hadn't been there, if I had done something different. If, If, If. Maybe this could have all been different. That keeps me stuck."

Oh, how I get that! I have had many accidents in my life. I have lots of scars to show from demonstrating too much daring or too little attention, or I just happened to be in the wrong place at the wrong time.

Close to 100% of the time, though, I look back and say, "Why did I do that? What was I thinking?" We humans tend to do that, to not notice the potential consequences of things — which is why we have accidents. And it is why we are sometimes in the wrong place at the wrong time.

And there are plenty of times when I was involved in an accident, and there is no way I could have or should have seen it coming. I was doing all the right things, but something wrong still happened.

That is what keeps us stuck playing the "If only..." game. But, there is another game: "It DID happen. Now what?"

Acceptance can be tough on several fronts. First, acceptance means accepting we might have something to do with an event. That can be tough. Second, acceptance means realizing you don't have control over everything. We like to think we have more control. But, in reality, we have very little. And third, acceptance means we have to acknowledge living in a world where random events happen. That bumper sticker, "Sh** Happens" — it is pretty accurate.

But good stuff happens, randomly, too. We sometimes miss that. We don't notice all the moments where something bad *does not* happen. We don't always notice all the moments where something good *does* happen. Our fixation on the bad things is a survival mechanism. It just tends to limit our thriving.

Instead of playing the "If only..." game, let's shift to the "It happened, now what?" game. It is far more helpful and far more instructive. One keeps you stuck; the other allows you to grow and thrive.

"How do I know I am even making progress? It just seems that sometimes I am spinning my wheels."

First, I do have a core belief that when we get out of our own way, the healing process happens naturally. To be a bit graphic, if you cut or scrape yourself and you keep picking at the injury, it can't heal. You keep re-injuring the injury. But if you just allow the natural process, it generally heals. The same is true in life.

In fact, there are many emotional hurts and scrapes that we naturally allow to heal. We don't even notice the process. For example, if someone hurts your feelings, you might quickly realize they are not in a good place. You might even notice that you had some role in that event. And you might even learn a lesson, even if it is as simple as saying, "When I see that expression/tone/attitude, I will keep my distance." In other words, you might just run right through the steps and not even notice — and the hurt heals.

So how do you know you are making progress? Well, if you share my belief, you will trust that if you are intentionally trying to forgive, then you are making progress. If you are walking through the steps, you trust there is progress. Even slow progress.

Sometimes, the process can feel draining. Sometimes, it can feel slow. You might feel like you are slogging through. But remember, even then you are moving forward. Our biggest growth almost always comes from the biggest struggles.

For now, trust that if you are working the steps, there is progress. Then look for the signs (and listen to others who might see the signs) of progress.

"Okay, I have worked through the Forgive Process. I think I have forgiven. What should I be feeling? What will be different? How will I know I was able to forgive?"

Years ago, I suffered a fairly rare autoimmune illness. When it started, we didn't know what was going on. Between my stubborn refusal to see a doctor for several weeks and the rarity of my illness (along with some typical viral symptoms), we didn't know what was happening.

I only knew one thing: I was getting sicker and sicker. My body was weaker, hurting more, and my energy level was dropping day-by-day. Thanks to over-the-counter pain relievers, I managed to drag myself to work and home each day, but that was about it.

After several visits, my family doctor figured it out. He told us I would likely be disabled and it would eventually kill me. Those were tough words to hear. But I was fortunate. The type of illness I had was acute and not chronic. A specialist was the one who told me, four months into my illness, that I would eventually recover. It would take a while, though. By the time I saw the specialist, I was actually starting to feel better.

At about the six-month mark, I was starting to regain my strength. But I didn't always notice it directly. Sometimes, it was in the midst of doing something that I realized I was able to do it. In the midst of moving around, I realized I was not tearing up in pain. My shoes started fitting again as the swelling abated.

In other words, there was not an instant when I "recovered." The recovery took months. And I still have some residual joint pain, so I still "remember" the tough times. I just don't remember them as often or as vividly. Every now and then, I rub a joint and realize there is a bit of residual hurt. Then, I move on.

Some people work through the Forgive Process and feel like a weight has been lifted. Since the process is not instantaneous, you can't expect the change to be instantaneous. But there is a substantial shift throughout the process.

Others, though, realize the forgiving by noticing the lack of prior feelings. Maybe they feel less reactive around certain dates, places, or people. Maybe that tired feeling of dragging around something heavy begins to lighten. Energy begins to return. Anger dissipates. Hurt heals.

Many people tell me that others note it first. People ask them what is different. Perhaps they see a different demeanor. Perhaps they see smiles and hear laughter. They may notice a lighter countenance.

That is the process of forgiving — thawing out long-frozen emotions and allowing joy to resurface. But it can take a while.

Just accept that you are doing what you can to free yourself and let the process take care of the rest. You are designed to thrive. Forgiving lets you move in that direction.

Endings & Beginnings

Those are the 6 steps in the Forgive Process:

1. Decide to Forgive
2. Shift from Enemy to Empathy
3. Breathe and Release
4. Examine Your Role
5. Learn the Lessons
6. Re-Decide to Forgive

You now have a process you may use over and over in your life. Perhaps there is a major event or central person in your life that needs to be forgiven — not for the person's sake or even for the event, but for you. When you unlock forgiveness, you untie yourself from the events; you have a chance to let go of roles that no longer serve you.

The choice is yours. It always has been. Maybe you suspected that, but didn't know how to forgive. Or, maybe you didn't see a choice. At this point, I hope you see a new path forward.

No longer is it just a possible choice. There is a path. It's always been there, perhaps just a bit hidden.

When I was young, a group of us went on a hike through a wilderness area. When we gathered in the parking lot, our guide met us at a shaded corner. He told us about the trail we would follow. At places, he told us, it was simply a game trail. Animals ran through, leaving a small path. At other spots, the path would be clearly marked.

With that, he turned and pointed toward a "path." I saw nothing but brush. He pointed again. And as I looked closer, I finally spotted the slightly clearer section. I trusted that the guide had walked this way before, so I pushed through and followed. As we went, there were several times I could not see a path. The guide pointed it out again, and it became evident.

At times, I had no need for the guide; the path was fairly wide and clear. Just when I thought I had it, the trail would disappear — at least to me. The guide never lost track of it. He simply pointed us back to it when we were searching.

The guide didn't carry anyone down the path. He also didn't force us down the path. He pointed it out and let us follow it.

The path was there long before we arrived. And it was more clearly defined by the time we moved through. Just because I lost track of it from time to time didn't mean the trail wasn't there.

When I signed up for the hike, I decided to go. I committed to the hike, even when I wasn't convinced we could get through the woods. And several times, I pondered turning back. But I kept choosing to move forward.

We arrived on the other side, safe and secure. And I learned a bit more about picking through the woods, following a path, and pushing through. It was up to me. I just needed the guide to point the way through when the path got faint.

The path to forgiving is there for you. I can point it out. But the only way to benefit from the journey is to take it yourself. You don't have to know the trail to follow it, as long as someone can point it out to you when you aren't sure about the next section.

First, you choose to forgive. After that, take it a step at a time. At the other side of the process is a clearing. The process might feel dark and overgrown. Keep a watch for the path and trust the process.

When you emerge on the other side, you will discover healing, freedom, and power. All because you chose to not be bound by events or by the actions of another. You now have a choice. Staying stuck is not an option if you want to thrive.

This is the beginning of being unstuck. Let's get hiking.

About The Author

D r. Lee Baucom is a coach, consultant, therapist, author, and frequent speaker. In his work, Dr. Baucom strives to help individuals, couples, families, businesses, and organizations to thrive. For several decades, Dr. Baucom has helped individuals transform their lives and thrive.

The author of a number of books, including *Thrive Principles*, *The Immutable Laws of Living*, and *How To Save Your Marriage In 3 Simple Steps*, Dr. Baucom provides practical steps to create a thriving life.

You can learn more about Dr. Baucom and his work at http://LeeBaucom.com

If you would like to contact Dr. Baucom for coaching, consulting, or speaking, you can contact him here:

Aspire Coaching
4949 Brownsboro Rd., #147
Louisville, Kentucky 40222
502-802-4823
Lee@Thriveology.com

Morgan James
Speakers Group